FINE
COTTON
& ME

FINE COTTON & ME

The confessions of Hayden Haitana
AS TOLD TO GRAHAM BAUER

ANGUS & ROBERTSON PUBLISHERS

ANGUS & ROBERTSON PUBLISHERS
Unit 4, Eden Park, 31 Waterloo Road,
North Ryde, NSW, Australia 2113, and
16 Golden Square, London W1R 4BN,
United Kingdom

This book is copyright.
Apart from any fair dealing for the
purposes of private study, research,
criticism or review, as permitted
under the Copyright Act, no part may
be reproduced by any process without
written permission. Inquiries should
be addressed to the publishers.

First published in Australia
by Angus & Robertson Publishers in 1986

Copyright © John Stainton and Graham Bauer 1986

National Library of Australia
Cataloguing-in-publication data.
Haitana, Hayden.
　Fine Cotton and me.
　ISBN 0 207 15417 1.
　　1. Haitana, Hayden. 2. Fraud—Queensland. 3. Horse-
　racing—Queensland. 4. Racehorse trainers—
　Queensland. 5. Fine Cotton (Race horse). 6. Bold
　Personality (Race horse). I. Bauer, Graham. II.
　Title.

364.1' 63

Typeset in 11/12 pt Bembo by Midland Typesetters.
Printed in Australia

CONTENTS

	FOREWORD	vii
Chapter One	THE BOOT	1
Chapter Two	TED	5
Chapter Three	STAN	11
Chapter Four	KIWI	17
Chapter Five	A CHAINSAW MASSACRE	25
Chapter Six	FRED	31
Chapter Seven	EDDIE	33
Chapter Eight	MURPHY AND PETE	39
Chapter Nine	SANTANA	49
Chapter Ten	BAINSEY	53
Chapter Eleven	REAL CHAMOZZLE	61
Chapter Twelve	APPRO	69
Chapter Thirteen	THE PHANTOM	81
Chapter Fourteen	FINE COTTON	87
Chapter Fifteen	BUNDAMBA	95
Chapter Sixteen	MORTAL LOCK	99
Chapter Seventeen	BOLD PERSONALITY	109
Chapter Eighteen	DIXON	119
Chapter Nineteen	SILVERTONGUE	125
Chapter Twenty	EAGLE FARM	133
Chapter Twenty-one	THE RACE	139
Chapter Twenty-two	THE PAY OFF	145
Chapter Twenty-three	FAME	151
Chapter Twenty-four	THE FALL OUT	159
Chapter Twenty-five	MANDY	165

FOREWORD

Knowing Hayden Haitana is an addictive form of self-punishment. Neither his company nor his life story are for the lily livered. Throughout almost a year of researching this book, much of it in Hayden's company, I felt my emotional reserves dwindling and my liver enlarging at alarming rates.

During the first week alone I saw Hayden run bravely to the scene of a fight and begin attacking the aggressor, only to discover he was a male nurse whose patient was throwing a fit; I watched him con close associates into a hopeless horse deal; I saw him drink the pants off an attractive young reporter.

As Hayden himself puts it, "Some have a weakness for drink, some for women, some for the punt and some for the con — but I'm lucky. I got the lot." And after months of watching him in action I found myself giving a frightening credibility to his outrageous stories of life as a confidence man. I made a swift decision to change names to protect the innocent.

And when the writing was over and I was watching him being taken away to jail in November 1985, I thought about him this way: Hayden Haitana is a man of warmth, humour and surprising intelligence. It's just that he's never *ever* to be taken seriously.

Graham Bauer

Chapter One
THE BOOT

I might have been at a beach, surrounded by sweaty, sunbaking bodies, except for the chickenwire stretched across the sky and the fact that cement is tougher on the back than sand. The prisoners lay side by side on the slab, basking like lizards, crammed into a room-sized cage with enough space to mind their own business and no more. And how I wished they would. Cons pestering me for autographs and cons pestering me for new, inside versions of how the Fine Cotton scam went wrong bored me mindless, there in Brisbane's Boggo Road jail, waiting for the Phantom to bail me out.

Day after day his messages said the bail would be through tomorrow, and every night I was locked up again, disappointed. Fourteen grand was a lot to raise but Gillespie — the Phantom — could whisk up bail like a packet pudding when it suited him, so I could only assume that for some twisted reason he wanted me in cold storage. Not that jail was too bad, but I was keen to keep an eye on developments outside, because for sure Gillespie and the Cotton crew would be working on something new, something outrageous, and they weren't the kind that asks permission before dragging you into a con so deep you can't get out.

"Hayden Haitana to the office!"

The loudspeaker boomed and as the relief surged through me, I noticed a different sound in the compound, a sort of buzzing which put the guards on edge. It grew steadily as I was escorted between the pens into administration, hoping like hell that this wasn't another false alarm.

"Bail's paid," said the duty officer.

"At last!"

"That's right. Get your stuff together and report to the gate. And listen, there's another thing. Whoever paid up has tipped off the press. There's hundreds of the bastards waiting outside."

I laughed, well used to the media by now. I was interested to know why the Phantom had called in the cameras but not overly worried. The way I saw it, the main thing was getting out, and a quick news conference was a small price to pay for it.

But when the Cotton boys are operating nothing is ever that simple, and what's worse, nothing ever seems to work. As I collected my belongings from the cell the whap-whap-whap of a helicopter drifted over the courtyard, and a muttering started — a rumble from the prisoners which quickly grew to a roar. I rushed out to the balcony, where the duty officer was peering skyward.

"What's that?"

"It's a bloody chopper, but they've got no business here, I can tell you! It's restricted airspace."

The machine, a colourful T.V. news job with a camera lens poking from a side window, circled lazily, whipping the prisoners into a frenzy. They screamed at it, and waved, and shook the chickenwire. It looked like my two hundred metre walk to the main gates was going to be a bit of a gauntlet. As soon as I hit the yard the pens erupted.

"Haitana's going out!"

"They sent a chopper for him!"

"Hay-den Hay-den Hay-den!"

The animal roar from hundreds of male throats and the sea of blue prison shirts were frightening, and had the potential to become a full-scale riot. The guards tensed, hands on their guns, and I cursed the Phantom roundly.

"I'll wring his bloody neck!" I fumed, breaking into a trot.

My solicitor felt much the same. He was already at the security gates, frantic, waving me toward the open boot of a car. I couldn't wait to get out of there, flinging my suitcase into the boot and rushing around to the front passenger door.

"Hold up, Hayden!" he shouted over the racket. "You've got it wrong!"

"What?"

"Throw your suitcase in the back. The boot's for you. Otherwise we'll never get past the mob outside."

"What, the media? But Gillespie set it up!"

"Well, if he did he's changed his mind. Quickly, hop in now."

"I'll suffocate! You could've brought a Falcon or something!"

His car was a tiny four cylinder hatchback job, and it looked like a tight squeeze.

"Just get in will you? We're only going to the closest pub."

That magic word! I would have been happy to jump into the boot of a mini! I crawled in, pushing the back seat slightly forward to give a bit of ventilation, and a crack to peep through.

The gates opened, and a few moments later I heard the media shout go up.

"I should get twice the fee for this," the solicitor snapped, and the car slowed to walking pace, hampered by a crush of bodies around us.

I watched the blur of tense faces and cameras shoved at the windows, and couldn't help a huge grin. I almost shouted "Help! Help! I'm being kidnapped!" to stir them up a bit, but my chauffeur beat me to the punch.

"You want Haitana, don't you?" he said calmly. "He's in the next car."

I hugged myself with glee, hoping that the next car would be full of cops. Disappointed, the press blockade parted muttering four letter words, and we were home free.

But how many times had I said exactly that, "home free", only to discover than an unforeseen disaster waited around the next bend? All my life I seemed to have been involved in some crazy scam or another, and whether I got away with it or not, something always went terribly wrong at the very last moment.

Of course, I reasoned, everything that could possibly go wrong with the Fine Cotton ring-in already had. In that sad case, something went wrong every single moment until it finally crashed in a desperate, screaming bloody heap. In fact far, far, far too much had gone wrong. Enough to make me think that maybe, at the end, it had turned into a full scale set up — a sting, then a double, then a triple, and then worse. It got so bad, so ridiculous, so tangled, so bloody hopeless, that only the Phantom could have convinced us to push on regardless.

He was that good, Gillespie, one of the best in the business; a handsome, stocky man with pale blue eyes and an incredibly cheeky grin that made you sure you could trust him. When the Phantom grins, the most hard-baked, suspicious, seasoned confidence men go gooey ... and suckers like me don't stand the ghost of a chance.

"You just leave it to me, Haitch, and everything will be all right!" he had grinned, time after time, and I believed him. That's why I was where I was, jammed in the boot of a car, having been charged with a multimillion dollar conspiracy to swap one racehorse for another, and firmly locked into that old cycle—bail, committal, trial, and whop! Back in jail. Freedom-bound as the car took a corner and accelerated uphill, I turned my mind to what plans the Phantom might have made for me in the meantime.

There was no doubt that a scheme would be on the boil to finance our legals, and there was a fair chance that Gillespie was using my name to sell it. The Fine Cotton publicity had given me sudden status in the underworld—the kind that gets you access to closed circles and up-front money, and the Phantom just couldn't resist such an opportunity. More than that, using my name would be a good way of trapping me into a con, because if there's heavy money involved, and you're known to be in on it, you can't back out without making folks plenty angry. That is how the Phantom operated. He might have been slapdash in detail, but he was very careful with overall structure. His scams were set up so that if ever anyone blew the whistle, the whole shebang came crashing down around them, and cops, crims, and victims all pointed the finger of blame directly at the blabber. Once you're on that crazy rollercoaster ride with Gillespie, you can scream all you like but you can't get off.

But if that was the case, another little one couldn't hurt, a little inoffensive one for old time's sake—not after a career of surviving all kinds of mayhem and con. Fresh out of jail, on the way to meet the Phantom, I could feel that other old snake, temptation, slithering under my skin, and the sensation was delicious. Once the con gets into your blood it's a cool customer and a hard bugger to shake. And it's the people as much as anything that keep you in the game; the gutsy, the light-fingered, the larcenous, often meaning well enough in their own twisted ways. But as the parson says, the road to hell is paved with good intentions, and I know better than anyone that it's a steep and slippery downhill slide.

Chapter Two
TED

To select accurately the point where my life went terribly wrong is like trying to make a smart decision on pools numbers—hopeless. The variety of events and combinations of events is endless, but the steepest plunge probably came with an Aussie bastard called Ted, and the drunken disaster of my migration from Kiwi to Australia.

I was visiting my mother just outside Lake Taupo on New Zealand's North Island, all kitted out for holidays, my wallet well-stuffed, full of the adventure of a driving vacation with no special destination. I felt sort of heroic, like an explorer.

"That's nice," Mum said absently. "Quickly now, run into town and get me a bottle of milk."

It wasn't exactly the kind of heroism I had in mind, but luckily I ran into two fellow holiday-makers in Lake Taupo who proposed an honourable solution.

"Let's do a pub crawl."

"Get really pissed."

"All right, all right!" I agreed. "But I've got to be home for an early night."

"Sure thing, Haitch. Hi ho Silver!"

"Away!"

The car doors slammed with finality, and for three days the roads from Lake Taupo to Wellington were hazardous, the three of us roaming from pub to pub, drinking hard and terrorising innocent female citizens with offers of permanent relationships.

At last, when we realised we were too paralytic to handle our rusty steed, deliverance came in the form of a lanky Aussie. Ted was a hitchhiker whose offer to take the wheel was a matter of self-protection, but he was quickly as out of it as we were, and worried as hell because he had some special air fare organised out of Wellington the following day. Time after time, in pub after pub, we had to promise on our honour we'd get him there in time and in one piece.

"Don't you worry, Ted, you big bronzed bloody Anzac," I growled. "We'll make it. But now we gotta stay for a few more 'cause the barmaid's in love with me."

The barmaid was not in love with me. She was so out of love with me she cracked me in the side of the head with a beer mug, but we were made of pretty stern stuff and the crawl continued unabated.

No one was more surprised than me when we kept our promise, arriving in Wellington hours early, in gushing rain. Drunk, loud, tired and emotional, we entered into a beery pub squabble over Kiwi's weather.

"A duck'd get footrot over here!" bitched the Australian.

"How would you know? Aussie bastard!"

"I know. You oughta come over to Aussie and see some real weather!"

"Well, I might," I slurred, "and it better be good!"

It was just raving but the pace of drinking was furious. I was already smashed, more drinks were lined up, and the next I remember, my friends were waving me goodbye at the airline gate.

"He has decided to make a new life," dribbled one.

"I bags the car."

"I've got his shotgun."

I was sound asleep when the plane touched down and I woke in a muddle. I stared around at people struggling from their seats into a queue, muttering, pushing, and tugging briefcases down from the lockers. On a loudspeaker someone thanked me for something. The pouring rain made me guess this was Wellington, but I couldn't come to terms with the aeroplane business and the rush, or why the man beside me seemed somehow familiar.

"Sorry about the rain," Ted said. "You musta brought it with you."

I gave him the once over. "Ted?" I croaked, and he nodded.

"The same."

"Where are we?" I looked through the window at tarmac workers being bashed senseless by solid sheets of rain.

"Sydney, mate. Home of Kings Cross."

I slumped in the seat as the memories bubbled to the surface — the pub, the bold decision, the hangover, the no sweaters.

"It's freezing. Where am I going to live?"

"With me. We'll get a flat up the Cross."

I was cold, nineteen, and I had a headache. I was unemployed, unskilled and naive, and within a few days I was taken by every pimp, whore, con and thief in Kings bloody Cross.

It became apparent I had landed in a very juicy slice of Australia when the real estate man showed us the first flat on our list of prospectives.

"You'll love it!" he glowed. "It's got new furniture, new paint, new everything!"

He flung wide the door and watched eagerly for our reactions, but the place was bare — not a stick of furniture, not a loop of carpet, not even a wall socket. The thief obviously took strong professional pride in his work, so Ted and I nodded respectfully at each other, looked at the agent's dumb gape, and roared with laughter.

"Bastards! Bastards!" choked the salesman, and we weren't sure whether he meant them or us.

But just half an hour later our grins were wiped away. We had picked up the keys to another flat and, after propping my new suitcase against the door to keep it open against the breeze. I trotted back to the footpath for some of Ted's gear. Seconds later, I heard the door slam.

"That's odd," I said. "My case was holding that open."

Ted looked at me, and I looked back. A shiver rolled down my spine and we sprang to action, bolting upstairs to discover that my suitcase was gone. I stared around in mute rage, and a slim trace of smile teasing Ted's face evaporated.

"Bastards," he spat.

"Bastards," I agreed spitefully, and Ted took me by the shoulders.

"Hayden, Hayden, Hayden. You heard of something called streetwise? It's when you're not a goose. The Cross is jam-packed with people on the lookout for a plumbum like you. You're easy pickings so you're gonna have to wise up quick. I'll tell you what I'll do. You stick with me, and old Ted'll show you the ropes, hey?"

Naive nineteen year olds place a lot of stock in pride, and advice is taken like the kind of foul cure-all tonic your mother forced on you when you were a kid.

"Let me handle it unless you can see I'm doing something really wrong," I suggested.

"You're gonna find yourself in all sorts of queer situations!" he smiled, and later I would regret being too dumb to pick up the inference.

My education started that same afternoon, on the main drag, where a shiny new car pulled up next to me with two hot-looking sorts in the front seat.

"Want a lift, honey?" said the blonde, and I gaped. As if I, Hayden Haitana, needed education!

"I'll see you round," I drawled to Ted, and climbed eagerly into the car. The smell of new upholstery mingled with shampoo and two brands of perfume, creating a heady atmosphere.

"Thirty dollars love," said the redhead.

I smiled back, uncomprehending.

"For the ride," winked the blonde, a well-stacked lass with softer features than her companion, who on close inspection had turned out to be a bit of a harpy.

After a moment of dumb confusion, I blushed hotly. "What? I could get a cab cheaper than that."

The women gazed back, uncertain whether I was trying to be smart or was fair dinkum stupid, and then Ted's face was at the window.

"They're pro's!" He was giggling helplessly. "They're bloody pro's!"

Humiliated, I struggled back onto the footpath and faced Ted with fury. "Well, why do they want to give me a bloody lift?"

He collapsed.

After I had fallen for a few minor confidence tricks and made fools of the pair of us, Ted began going to enormous lengths to protect my wallet. We were rarely apart, and he often alerted me to dangers I was then incapable of sensing. We might be drinking peacefully at some pub and out of the blue he'd be at my elbow, speaking softly from the corner of his mouth.

"Quick, mate. There's gonna be a fight. Let's get out of here!"

Personally, I wasn't all that worried about a blue or two, but I continued to accept his advice until at last it happened so frequently I got jack of it.

"It's on, Hayden. Those two blokes in the corner. Let's scram."

"Nah. Bugger it. They can kill each other as far as I'm concerned."

"Come on. Let's piss off."

"Can I buy you a drink?" a businessman type asked, and rather strangely Ted lit out, white-faced, without another word.

"Anything from the top shelf down!"

He was well spoken, well dressed, urbane, and seemed fascinated by anything I said, even long-winded stories of youthful hardship.

"See, one of my brothers and I had to share the same bed with a row of pillows between us, and . . ."

"The poor pillows!" he interrupted, and I noticed he was drinking something purple. On reflection, all of this did seem a trifle queer. There was a long pause in the conversation.

"Well," he said. "Off to my apartment?"

"What? What do you mean?"

His face grew taut. "You know what I mean."

"I'm bloody sure I don't!"

"Do I have to put the weights on your pimp!"

Whap! I flattened him. One punch. That bastard Ted had been flogging my behind to every old queer in the Cross, cash in advance, and it's no wonder he could always see a fight coming. I found "ol' Ted" up the road and gave him a hiding too, finishing up blind drunk at a nightclub. And when I returned to our flat, drunk, morose and depressed, he had cleared out with everything I owned. The night was freezing and my blankets were gone.

Too upset to sleep, I shivered alone in the silence of my poky little home, with no one to talk to and no one to telephone and nowhere to go. There was nothing to do but dwell on the battering my ego had taken, and struggle with rising anger and frustration. I looked from my window into a grubby Kings Cross street, still dotted with whores, and vowed that from that moment on I would be playing a tough game, by Ted's rules, and Australia had better watch out! The confidence career of Hayden Haitana had taken root, and swiftly began to bud.

First up, I pulled a few minor jobs around the Cross, borrowing money from out-of-towners and working under false pretences, but it was amateur stuff. Jaded by unpleasant memories and unnerved by the sickly, indoor pallor of the people, I couldn't seem to get motivated. When a circus came to town advertising for roustabouts, I jumped at the opportunity.

Chapter Three
STAN

A circus career meant putting the confidence game on hold before I had properly started, but if that was disappointing, there were compensations. In the belief that one day I would be famous for something, I tended to see my life in headlines and this one kind of grabbed me—"Haitana Runs Away—Joins Circus!" What's more, it was one of the few jobs available with a free roof, food and transport, and when you're broke, unskilled, and only have the one set of clothes that's a godsend. My part-Maori blood made me look more roustaboutish than average and I was strong, so getting the job was easy enough.

"Name?"

"Thomas . . . Hayden Thomas."

And I was on, working under an alias, which made me feel better. Life was on the up and it didn't take too long for the wonderful irrepressibility of circus life to get its hooks into me. I loved all things in which circus people find romance—the characters, caravans, mud, sawdust, soiled costumes, and ever-present smells of hide and dung. In fact, there was a roustabouts' game called "Hide and Dung", loosely based on flinging the stuff, but for sheer decency's sake we'll skip it. I had various work responsibilities but most of my time was spent hiding from work.

"Thomas! You bludger! When I find you I'll . . . .." The abuse rang loud and fruity across the site while I rested, swigging on a bottle under a casual arrangement of canvas.

And if I had believed my career as a con was on hold, working conditions soon woke me up. Management regarded itself as overly generous in doling out ten dollars a week and baked dinners—meaning baked beans. Beans, baked, every bloody meal! I like baked beans, but they get a bit much for the senses after a while—particularly for other diners in close proximity.

To eat properly, let alone drink properly, you needed cash, and my big endeavour was using any means possible to supplement my income. I didn't resent this because it was satisfying work and sharpened my wits, and in the end it gave me confidence because the scam I set up was a bang-on winner.

All the roustabouts were press-ganged into selling tickets to passing trade outside the gates, an odious task unless you could twist it to your advantage. They gave us enormous reels of those cheap "Admit One" numbers and I figured there was no chance anyone could keep tabs on how many were sold so I flogged them like a fishmonger, on my own behalf, at pubs and on the street.

"Roll on, roll on!" I shouted like a pro. "Half price to the circus the next twenty tickets!"

I also sold in bulk to enterprising salesmen who could make a good percentage while I sat like an entrepreneur, lunching at the pub. The manager, curse his soul, never understood why gate takings were down and the seats were full, and he watched us like a hawk. He didn't ever twig, and I made a good living, but damn it! after six glorious months, a nightmarish combination of events brought my circus career undone—a series of events which started with tigers.

I always got on well with animals but I hated tigers: they stank to high heaven and were so vicious you had to feed them off the end of a broom. One job I couldn't escape was herding the buggers from cage to cage so that I could clean up after them. For a start it meant getting dangerously close, holding my nose and sweating buckets, but on this certain night I was playing it cool for the benefit of a dangerously young honey blonde who seemed interested.

Apart from drink, women were my big weakness, and I would go to extraordinary lengths to impress. Circus romance was an uncomplicated affair because it was by nature short-lived. However this meant you had to move fast. So, feeling the blonde's sultry eyes on my back, I risked teasing the cats until they snarled, making me pooey with fright. But I recovered quickly, the honey blonde seemed to appreciate it, and our following conversation would have happened something like this:

ME: I caught that big bugger myself in India, but you know there's nothing like Africa. It's just magic at dawn, with a black tracker, hunting impala down by the Limpopo.
HER: I'm Penny.
ME: Oh, I'm used to the danger of course. I was a big white hunter until I hurt my back saving some guy from a croc.
HER: Hey! Can you get me in for free?

I had the dialogue off pat and she knew I was lying through my teeth. Penny probably had no particular interest in me, or the tigers for that matter, but free tickets were a powerful love potion. We were young, the night was starry, and the menagerie was our oyster. I remember feeling very gallant, there among the strings of bare bulbs and farty scents of the circus.

I described in detail the mating habits of every animal we encountered, and my imagination was fired up by then so it was a pretty steamy trip. I had to get to the point quickly because I had my own circus act to prepare—two ponies, two camels, and a savage troupe of monkeys experienced in all facets of gang warfare. It was a performance of my own invention. The camels lay down, the monkeys mounted the ponies (and sometimes each other) and the whole shebang ran in circles jumping the camels' humps while I cracked a whip.

It sounds simple enough but preparation was important because the monkeys were led by a vicious and cunning old buck called Stan (the originator of "Hide and Dung") and they tended to play up. Stan was a thief and a spitter, and his tribe, which looked up to him, tended to follow suit. Once, the bastards ran riot in the middle of my act, snarling, while I cracked my whip in an embarrassing parody of the previous lion-taming show. The audience went wild and I was livid, chasing Stan up the trapeze ladder for a showdown. He turned on me in mid-stride, but I beat him to the punch, landed a right hook fair in his maw, and only then did the other monkeys fall into line. Once you beat up the leader they lose heart, and it taught me the value of roughing them up just before we went on to make it clear who was boss.

"I think I love you," Penny was bound to have said as we wrestled beneath a wrap of canvas.

"And I love you," I was certain to have replied as the band struck up its opening number. In the wings nearby the elephants were waiting for their cue, all done up in bells and rugs, surrounded by the various performers—the clowns, acrobats and so on. Their cue was simple: music meant "walk" for the Grand Opening Parade. My job was also simple: I had to reef down on a rope halyard, parting the curtains of the performers' entrance as the parade swung into motion. But tonight I was preoccupied.

"Curtain!" the ringmaster bellowed. "The curtain!"

"Curtain?"

The warning came too late. I was tangled in a chaos of canvas and female, desperate to move and frozen in horror as the elephants shuffled forward. Their massive feet pinned down the curtain hems. They leaned forward into the cloth. Tent tore, poles snapped, wire pinged, performers screamed, the crowd shrieked with delight and the entire shemozzle of curtain collapsed on the cast. It was a bloody mayhem of struggling animals and stunned performers, with the audience in hysterics. I watched for a moment, fascinated by the consequences of my passion, but it seemed silly to wait around so I used the diversion to escape.

"Okay. That was definitely a mistake," I said to the night. Unless I could think of some way to put it right I was a cert for the sack. After a while it came: the perfect solution. I remembered the manager had been enraged when a rival cotton candy vendor set up outside the circus gates, because our own Kandy Karavan charged colossal prices and the competition was killing its trade. I reasoned that removing the cause had to be a job-saving coup for Hayden Thomas, and the plan was simple. As our rival wouldn't shift happily, force was necessary, and there were tons and tons of brute force right on tap in the Big Top—the elephants! The mess had been sorted out by then, so I pleaded with the handler who was a mate of mine, and in return for the promise of a six pack he eventually agreed.

When you carry a big stick and you know you're going to win it's easy to be nice, so I tried that first, approaching our friend like I wanted a bag of chips or something.

"Gidday!"

"Hey, you're from the circus!"

"That's the problem, mate. I won't be from the circus unless you piss off out of here, so now you better pack up or we'll shift you."

"Bugger off!" he said.

There was no time for further discussion as my reinforcements would shortly be needed back in the ring. The next our vending friend knew of it, the elephant had shoved his vehicle off its blocks and was pushing it steadily toward the road. It made a remarkable sight, the caravan carving big furrows in the grass. That's when the real trouble started because the owner was threatening to shoot the beast with a .22 rifle and we jeered at him. The prospect of fronting an elephant with a peashooter was laughable, but he got so dirty he ducked off, brought the gun back, and fired it into the air.

Elephants do not respond well to gunshot, and ours trumpeted away across the site. There was frenzy and fearful panic before the animal was caught and pacified, and I was back where I started, sweaty and feeling sick. By the time the drama died the offending caravan was also back where it started and it was the vendor laughing. But somehow, when the police had come and gone the circus owner found it in his heart to forgive me. It was the frame-up a few nights later that sealed my fate.

Some troublemaker had been coming around at night and letting the animals loose and, while the cops had been alerted, all of us had to take turns at guard duty. When my shift started I was drunk as usual. I was giving the cage doors a good shake to make sure they were secure, when a massive copper jumped me from behind. I was face down in the mud before I could argue and he jammed a pair of handcuffs on me tight enough to hurt.

"Gotcha, ya bastard!" he yelled, and called for his partner.

"No mate, you've got it all wrong!" I groaned. "I work here!"

"Yeah, yeah."

I was furious and put up a fight, shouting for help and trying to break loose, but it was futile. It was worse than futile, because when the circus manager was called to the station to identify me the police gave me the treatment.

"This bloke's a real animal," said the arresting officer. "Put up a hell of a struggle."

"Yeah, he's one of ours. A real trouble maker too," the manager said. "This time he's gone too far. Thomas, you're out. Sacked."

"Listen, you couldn't loan me ten bucks for the drunk and disorderly fine, could you? I promise I'll clear out in the morning and that's fair dinkum."

The manager grinned evilly. "No, bugger it. It'll teach you a lesson."

One telephone call was then all that stood between me and a miserably lonely night in the watch-house, and considering it was already midnight I didn't hold much hope.

"Ah . . . Mrs Clarke? Sorry to wake you, it's Hayden here. Can I speak to Christine?"

"Hayden? What's wrong?"

"See, I'm in a little bit of trouble at the cops, and I need ten dollars or they'll lock me up all night."

"Oh . . . well, okay. I'll get Chris up and send her down with the car."

I could scarcely believe it! Christine was a bright young thing, a real softy who had invited me home to dinner a few nights back. Her mother was freshly divorced and the three of us had celebrated gaily. I smirked away the next twenty minutes with fantasies involving the rest of the night.

Soon Christine, her face scrubbed of cosmetics and still druggy with sleep, was looking up at me as I paused on the stairs to savour the sight of her. She was the sweetest woman I had ever been released into the custody of.

"Where are you going to go?" she asked a few minutes later, on the footpath outside the station.

I hung my head. "Probably sleep in some park. But don't worry, love, I'll be all right."

"Mum says you can stay with us, but you've got to do it with her."

"What? I hardly know the woman!"

"It's that or nothing."

Romance put a gun to its head and pulled the trigger. But what's a man to do? Sleep in a bloody park? At least it was warm, there was food in the pantry, and I could always say that my circus career ended with a bang.

Chapter Four
KIWI

Whether you're at the mercy of a gay divorcee or the Phantom, there's no such thing as getting out of jail free. The code of the con says you're in debt and have to pay in return favours, because that's how the kind of people who get out of jail like it. And when they call in the debt, the job they want you to do always sounds simple and harmless, when it's nearly always complex and illegal as hell. You just end up doing other people's dirty work, and that's why the Phantom was always so far ahead of us. I knew how to take advantage of situations okay, but I always did the job myself, while Gillespie knew how to take advantage of people and they ended up doing all the nasty work for him.

The car braked hard and I overbalanced with a thump.

"Sorry about that!" the solicitor said. "You right?"

"Yeah, I wasn't thinking. Only about Johnny G."

He paused as the car accelerated again, and I pushed the back seat further forward to listen.

"Yes, do yourself a favour and watch that crowd, will you?" he advised. "You're in enough strife as it is."

"You know the Phantom at all?"

"Not really. Sounds like a larrikin though."

"You're not kidding. The bugger gets everyone in the shit before you know it. He had some bloke down at the penthouse on the coast a few weeks ago, just a straight business meeting, and now the poor bastard's probably up to his neck in it."

"How do you mean?"

"He works it this way, see. He makes sure he runs into this bloke a few days later and says: 'That receptionist at the units is hot for you.

She was full of questions after you left.' Then he says he can set up a date for this bloke. The guy can't remember the receptionist and the problem is he's married with a pregnant wife so he says 'No thanks'. But as soon as he tells the Phantom about his family, Johnny knows the bugger's hooked, because he wouldn't mention it otherwise."

"His marriage? How does Gillespie figure that?"

"Well, he reckons the bloke's really talking to himself, reminding himself about his responsibilities, so beneath it all he's got to be interested. John drops the subject to let the bloke stew on it, and next time the poor bastard comes down to the coast, there'll be some pro pretending to be the receptionist and he's gone. Especially after a few drinks."

"What's Gillespie got to gain?"

"That's the interesting part. Nothing at the time, but this bloke's straight, see? And you never know when you're going to need someone to front for something—someone the cops don't know. And Gillespie never has to mention the receptionist thing again. The bloke just knows he's got to keep Johnny sweet, and by the time he cottons on to the size of the deal he's been stung into, it's too late to do anything but go along."

"Did this fellow fall for it?"

"Don't know, but going by past experience, I reckon."

"Look, just duck your head, Hayden. There's a truck going to pull up beside us and this must look a bit odd."

Bloody Gillespie and his bloody schemes! "What's his weakness?" he would ask himself aloud. "Women? Money? The punt?"

The punt was another beauty. The Phantom would provide hot tips from the S.P. bookmakers until his prospects knew they were as close as you get to a sure thing and started to bet in big lumps. Next came a string of shockers, dead lasts, but it usually took a few major losses before his victims backed off the punt, and by then they were desperate to get their money back and they'd do just about anything. Of course, Johnny always had something a little bit illegal in mind for them. In fact the Phantom was so confident of human weakness he would even warn his punters of the dangers, but that only made them trust him more when the betting rainbow collapsed.

I suffered all the major human weaknesses and more, but mainly laziness, so the Phantom was able to convince me that I was too damn smart to work. I was the perfect pigeon because I had suspected that very same thing from a very early age.

I grew up tough in a farm family of nine on the inhospitable slopes of Raetihi on the North Island of New Zealand. We worked the place pretty hard, but the cold got too much for Dad so he gave the farm away and moved down to timber country looking for work at sawmills in the Waikata area. After a brief stint at technical college (abandoned because my scholarship wouldn't support a growing fondness for drink) I joined the family there, took up bike riding to keep myself fit, and was soon obsessed by it. Within a few years I was a cert for New Zealand's Olympic cycling team, able to give the juniors an entire lap start; the coach reckoned I was a good chance for a medal. It was then that the "too smart to work" rot set in.

"Now you listen, Hayden!" my coach railed. "You've got a chance thousands would kill for, to represent your country at the peak of sporting competition and win! Your name could be a household word and you never know what career opportunities it might open up. But it doesn't come easy and it takes a hell of a lot more work than you're putting in now."

The fame and the career stuff sounded great, but I wasn't too excited about the "it doesn't come easy" bit.

"She's right, coach. I've got a special strategy!"

I sometimes wonder if, within myself, I set out to wreck my one big chance of proper fame, because some people are dead-set frightened of winning. But my secret Olympic training strategy was, in all probability, built out of sheer bloody sloth. The plan revolved around a road race which was big in the lead-up to selection, and I spent much less time training under guidance in favour of the "patented Haitana road racing technique", the schedule depending on how many cars negotiated a fearfully steep section of mountain highway near the end of the course.

I would wait at the summit for a vehicle to pass, give it a good head start, then launch off in pursuit, the object being to overtake. As a training technique dovetailed with my race strategy—to stay with the tail-enders taking it easy until we hit the downhill and then, while everyone else was braking, to go hell for leather and work up an unbeatable lead. There were risks involved but it would save work and it would be okay on the day if only fate was kind. Even then I should have realised the odds against fate smiling on a Haitana were very high, and today I still wonder what it is about me that gets right up the noses of the punting gods.

"It's Haitana again," they might have said. "Will we give the poor bastard a break?"

"He'd have to be hopeful, wouldn't he?"

"Yeah, that's right. Let's break his bloody neck!"

Naturally, on the morning in question it was pouring rain so hard that the race was nearly canned. I was all in favour of that, but the events schedule was tight and the committee grudgingly gave the thumbs up, with a warning for competitors to take it easy. The thought of the downhill tactic in those conditions gave me the willies, but I was committed — the race couldn't be won on fitness so it would have to be won on guts. Even the earlier stages were fogged in and dangerously slippery, but all was according to plan and I was running well back and rested when we hit the crest, the road a twisting, shining black snake below us, the leaders already slanted over into the first bend. I pedalled like a madman, bulleting past the field, cornering at stupid angles, and then everything went rather odd, in slow motion. It was nice, the sensation of flight, the knowledge that the effort was over. I landed hard, and the back injury still bothers me, but I remember the accident and the end of my cycling career in the same terms as I remember just about every challenge I've ever undertaken — I was ahead when I went down.

In search of a new diversion, I took a sudden interest in horseracing. One of my elder brothers was a strapper at the time, and I spent hours of good drinking time arguing that if someone tried to train me the way they trained horses I wouldn't perform for them. I argued that the modern techniques used by cyclists could work equally well on horses, and my brother became so bored with it all he got me a job in his stables.

This was at Rotorua with a trainer named Joe, a topnotch boozer who gradually spent less time with his horses and more at the pub. I had given him the impression that I knew a little something about training, so he left it to me and concentrated instead on cultivating his growing interest in drink.

The man was obviously moonstruck, but if I didn't make some attempt to fill his shoes the stable would disintegrate, so each morning

I arrived at the course riding one mount and leading two others, to issue instructions to the track riders. They thought I was nuts, because the strategies were idiotic and I didn't know the correct track lingo, but as the orders came "from Joe" they followed them as far as was practical. First, I figured that since none of the horses was doing well, a change was as likely to improve them as it was to cause harm, and those nags sure got change. Stayers sprinted and sprinters stayed, and the times actually improved. After a few weeks at the helm I was brave enough to give the more docile fellows a bit of a hit out myself, gradually gathering a powerful mess of awfully misplaced confidence.

One morning after a session I was riding back past the airport as usual when a little light aircraft buzzed in low over the trees and my charges took fright. The two I was leading split away in different directions and mine charged straight up the bitumen, sending the traffic into howling chaos. I howled too. A horse trying to run on bitumen is like a car trying to corner on ice. His feet slid violently as he spooked from cars at full gallop and it seemed safest to give him his head. I dropped the reins and hung like a leech to his mane but that was worse and would have resulted in death had I not jumped from his back and landed on the tarmac with a sickening crunch. I sat up painfully in the middle of an intersection, cars arranged at awkward angles all around me, with no sign of Joe's expensive mounts anywhere. There was no way I could tell him, but he was well on the way down the shute by then. He didn't notice that his star prospects were missing for three days. In the meantime I searched the newspapers for headlines like "Horse Motor Tragedy", and combed Rotorua by cycle.

And then it became impossible to cover for Joe, because he disappeared without trace. In fact not even his wife has seen him since—and the owners he was training for appeared to regard me, little more than a school kid, as being now totally responsible. For my part, I was well aware that my training was hardly up to professional standards and I dreaded the day when my charges were expected to perform. The crunch came, as it was bound to, when the owners instructed my brother to take the hot prospects to a carnival at Auckland, and I found myself charge of three Haitaina-trained entries on race day. My blood ran cold but I did the best I could, taking them through the procedures, hyping the jockeys, avoiding the owners and outlining race strategy. All the while, imaginary race calls kept echoing in my head—"Last! Last! By a staggering twenty lengths!"

The first bugger won hands down—walked it in—and I was more shocked than anyone. But by the time our third entry picked up second I was strutting around like an expert, knowing the prize money was big, drooling over the juicy bonus certain to be coming my way. I greeted the owners as equals, wreathed in smiles when they fronted at the stalls. One was waving a slip of paper which I assumed was the cheque but which wasn't.

"You little bastard! What's this?"

"A feed bill."

"I know it's a feed bill, you bloody fool! What I want to know is how you could use up a whole drum of molasses."

"The horses ate it."

"You're not trying to tell me they polished off a drum of the stuff in three days? Two pounds worth," he snapped, "and we're going to dock you!" I had come to the course with a pound to punt and had done extra well with it. There were now thirty pounds in my pocket and that made me brave.

"What am I supposed to know about horses? They wanted it, I gave it to them, they ate it, and bloody won! What more do you want?"

I was livid. I turned and stalked away.

"You come back here!" one shouted. "You load these horses up."

I turned back and pointed to the nasty one, a gelding which was a crazy son of a bitch.

"Watch out for that bastard! He'll bite your bloody arm off," I spat, and kept walking.

At sixteen years old I got blotto, unable to believe the ingratitude of it all. I did a job I was unqualified for, barely paid for, and had somehow pulled off one hell of a coup for bastards who could turn around and bitch about the price of molasses. No mention of the thousands of pounds they had won, just two pounds docked from my pay. I staggered off to the trots, put everything I had on the first race, and won, and won again, and from then on the night was a haze. All I remember is sharing a bottle of wine with a tramp in a park and giving him my suit in a fair trade. When my brother found me, semi-conscious at the railway station, I was wearing the tramp's rags, and still had fifty pounds in my pocket.

But it turned me off horse racing. I lost interest absolutely. Horses and everyone who dealt with them (apart from my brother) were bastards and it was a mug's game. It was a game for criminals and losers, and smart talk trackies, and shifty-eyed bookies and flouncy women in stupid hats. People talked about the vibrant colour of race meetings and I saw red. This Haitana was smart enough to know that racing was a right royal rip off, worthy of a wide, wide berth in future.

Chapter Five

A Chainsaw Massacre

But in time I chose to forgive the Sport of Kings, and I chose to trust a sneak like the Phantom, and I chose to be bundled out of prison in the boot of a car bound for a further con, all going to show that we Haitanas are a charitable lot with short memories and a terrible choice of friends!

"How did you get tied up with this bunch anyway?" asked the solicitor. "How did you get into this? We're going to have to go right through it from the beginning, you know."

"Are we nearly there?"

"Hold on to your horses! Sorry, bad joke. No, we're only two blocks from the jail."

"Is that right? Bloody hell! But can we leave the story 'til later?"

"Sure," he said. "Plenty of time."

But the answer to his question was simple enough. The one thing which made me a walk-over for the Teds and the Phantoms and a host of other cons was that I had discovered very early on that breaking the law can sometimes seem to be the right thing to do, and can even make a lot of people happy.

On one occasion one of my brothers and I were living in a small New Zealand town which boasted a twin village about thirty miles away. This twinship was a strained affair — fierce rivalry between Maori factions in each community turned the usual socials at the opposition's dance hall into bloodbaths, and the only practical solution was to build our own hall. But all of us were broke and for a long time the fighting continued, and worsened.

Initiative was scarce in that town, which suited me because if everyone was a loafer there was no reason to feel guilty about it. But after a really fierce tribal showdown it was agreed that something had to be done. It kicked off one afternoon in the pub when my brother took to organising — easy enough to do because everyone we needed was there. Two low-loaders were booked for 1 a.m. the following morning, at the site of an abandoned metal workshop on the edge of the opposing town. Timbercutters were instructed to be there with chainsaws, and a power worker was set up to lift certain backstreet lines from just after midnight. Labour was gathered in force.

"What about me?" I asked, fired up with enthusiasm.

"Ah," said my brother. "Hey, everyone, what can Hayden do?" There was silence.

"I know!" I said. "I'll handle the grog!"

The pub cheered and I glowed with pride. Now, that was a job I could be trusted with!

Late that night while the town slept we gathered our forces to steal an entire engineering workshop. It was sawn in half, loaded, transported through the back streets, rejoined out of sight of the road on a farmer's property, the lawns mowed, and all by dawn. The next night we held our first peaceful town dance. I was working in the pub at the time so booze and bands were made my business, and both were a breeze. When I booked bands for the hotel I made it a 3 a.m. finish and when they wound up at the pub at about 11 p.m., we all went off to the hall. In those days, beer was supplied to parties in tankers — they pulled up outside the function, ran lines inside, and a gauge showed how much had been drunk and that's what was charged for. When the hall needed drinks it was the simple matter of a little tinkering with the gauges, and Hayden was a popular man.

Eventually, when word got around, certain questions were asked, but no action was taken by the police. Breaking the law as a community was far more "proper" than as an individual, although I must admit that I was no stranger to the cops on either count. Over the years they chalked up a record twenty or so convictions for drink driving against me, but always seemed to go easy with the penalties because I did my best to put on an entertaining turn in court. The local magistrate, frustrated by yet another of my appearances and obvious disrespect for legalities, once asked me how I had travelled into town.

"I came by bus. And that's the honest truth!"

"Really, Mr Haitana? Where did you park the bus?"

There was an enormous burst of laughter, because it's compulsory to be amused if the magistrate makes a joke.

"Just up the road, Your Worship," I shot back, bringing the house down. Sadly, the police knew me well enough to take it seriously and I was followed. They must have watched me giggle as I strolled up the road, boarded the bus, and started it up, and a few minutes later I was back in court charged with unlicensed driving. But the one that landed me in the slammer was a shocker—a night packed with disaster—that dreaded night of the North Island Chainsaw Massacre.

In New Zealand's timber country, the size of a man's private parts is immaterial: it's the size of his chainsaw that counts. A man's chainsaw is sacred property, his best friend, and if it isn't a "bloody mongrel" likely to go crazy and rip his leg off at the thigh, it's gutless. At night the cutters lined them up in an old bicycle rack at the bar and argued endlessly about each others' tools, and as I had been earbashed by the same old stories for years I had learned more than enough to impress my own mates. The problem arose when, hearing second-hand of my "skill" with a chainsaw, old Mrs Khan cornered me into promising to lop this huge old tree of hers, and she got on my works about it because I kept putting it off until one fateful night at the timbercutters' pub, when at last I was drunk enough to get interested.

The borrowing of a chainsaw was a big responsibility but I was well known and well versed enough to get one of the cutters to agree. So after a few more beers with the old woman I found myself gearing up for the job. Chainsaws make a great sound—sort of "Pdrdrdrdr, Pdrdrdrdr, Vizzzzzz!' This one sliced into the trunk like it was melon and the sensation was delicious—it was the first time I had used such a powerful machine. But suddenly, inexplicably, it snuffed and jammed solid, and nothing would start it, and nothing would free it, and the night grew very cold. My eyes bulged. My heart pounded. My mouth dried. I could hardly expect to go back to the bar, tell this giant his mate was squashed under a couple of tonnes of tree, and expect to survive. I considered bashing it out with a sledge hammer, or pulling it out with a car, but neither were good solutions. The only way I could see of saving myself was to go back to the pub and borrow another chainsaw to cut it out.

I jammed that one as well, and the next, and the next, and it was coming on to closing time and those big, mean timbercutters would be starting to ask difficult questions like "Where's my chainsaw?"

"You lent it to Haitana, remember?"

"Hey—he borrowed mine too!"

"What's going on here. He took off with mine about half an hour ago!"

"What's the bastard up to?"

Any second they would come down the road in an ugly gang and kill me. And the forests were deep and dense in Waikata.

It's just the kind of drama which has always dogged me, and with the same old progression of events. First the favour, then the taking of certain harmless liberties, then the whole thing crashes and I'm in deep trouble. What's worse, it rarely stops there. I get angry about the injustice of it, can't think straight, and usually manage to make the situation even sorrier.

I was frantic, having used every trick I knew and several I invented on the spot to rip four massacred chainsaws out of the tree, when the timbercutters sprang me. They stared at their machines, quiet at first, going easy, taking plenty good time to get extra bloody mad. Then, sullen voices.

"Any other bastard would own up and get help. I could-a freed that in five seconds."

"Yeah, if there was a chainsaw left."

I stood, flush-faced, saying nothing in case that's what they were waiting for, but it got so ugly there was nothing to do but run for it. They were right on my tail as I leapt into the car, fumbled with the key, and accelerated hard. I knew the escape was only temporary, and I was right, because that's when things turned really bad.

I made town okay but I must have been weaving across the road, just crawling in the hope of avoiding attention, when this cop jumped out from nowhere, jammed his arm through the driver's window and tried to grab the keys. I panicked and hit the accelerator. He slipped on the bitumen. He got tangled in the steering wheel and ended up being dragged along the road by his arm, screaming blue bloody murder.

"Stop! For God's sake, stop!" he bellowed, his foot broken.

Trouble with a capital shit. I pulled up and drove the poor bugger to hospital but my charity didn't much impress the judge. He considered my record, my bloodshot eyes, and the injury I had caused to an officer of the law were more relevant to the case.

"I know I done wrong, Your Honour," I said with a tight smile, relying on his sympathy, but he chucked the book at me—jail. The only consolation was that since the whole nightmare started from trying to do a widow a favour, I reckoned something good would have come of it. As it happened, after the trial and sentencing, I met a man who was going to change my luck.

Chapter Six
FRED

I've never met anyone who reeked so much of Charles Dickens—a mixture of what's-his-name, the convict out of *Great Expectations*, and Fagan from *Oliver Twist*. Old, hardened, gentle, cunning, giving, Fred was a con's con. The Kiwi jails might be enlightened, but jails are jails the world over, hazardous for a young, athletic lad such as I, and Fred rode shotgun. God knows he was probably queer, but he was tough and didn't push the point and once that was clear he was all right by me. We had a great time at work camps in the mountains, where we'd steal the warder's lunch and the poor bastard nearly starved, and where Fred's outside mates left booze hidden for us. Sometimes we could barely stand, let alone work. We laughed and gambled for cigs and never kept count, and all the time Fred kept saying how he was going to change my luck.

"Problem with the world today is you young people gotta get a break or you're payin' somethin' off your whole bloody life and you don't get a chance to live proper. Not much fun for a young bloke now, far as I can see, but you'll be right because there's sumthin' you don't know about just yet."

And a few days before I was released, when we were sitting silent in our cell not wanting to talk about the parting of company, that grizzled old rascal told me where he had hidden a fortune, all the loots from the armed robbery that put him inside.

"I always said I'd be lucky for you, old stick," he grinned, "an' here's proof of the puddin', 'cause half of it's yours. It's sitting in the cockpit of that aircraft memorial thing at the airport. You just take your share and leave the rest for old Fred. And don't you say nothing, because you done me good with your company and it's a fair reward."

The hours dragged, the minutes crawled, the seconds limped, but so soon I was going to be rich. I spent the time nervously, working on how much I would be able to spend per year, per week, per day, for the rest of my life, never having to work again. I thought about investment and rates of interest. I dreamed about yachts and foreign cars and expensive dinners. I read up on Europe and America and chose holiday destinations. For three days I explored every fantasy a man could have, and then the gates were open and I walked out into a bright, beautiful, free, sunny afternoon.

I chose not to hurry, enjoying the experience, pausing for coffee at a cafe and a read of the afternoon tabloid. I was in ecstasy and it took a long time for the front page to sink in. But there it was, in black and bloody white.

That same morning, a boy had discovered a fortune in cash in the aircraft memorial at the airport, and turned it in to the police. Fred's fortune. My fortune. My mind went blank. I took my time over the coffee, then strolled across the road to the pub. One vodka, one beer, one vodka, one beer, and so on until closing, taking turns, one for me and one for poor old Fred. That incredible grubstake could have been a big turning point—but truthfully, probably not. It probably would have gone in loans to friends and gifts to women and income to the bookies and booze.

There's no cheating destiny. Mine was a layabout's life, and that's how I liked it, because that's how I was brought up. Money didn't mean anything much to my parents and it doesn't mean much to me, apart from sheer survival. My family, happy to offer support and advice instead of a whipping when I found myself in trouble, chose not to burden me with high expectations of success. And they filled me with faith in human nature and a sense of fun, and refused to pass on the kind of guilt which crushes so many free spirits.

Of course, there is one powerful disadvantage to my kind of upbringing. People like me, people who don't suffer much from feelings of guilt, can't resist temptation, and that means we're suckers for the con.

Chapter Seven
EDDIE

I felt in my pocket for the letter and held it up to the light. It was covered in crayon hearts and the solicitor, watching in the rear-view mirror, was obviously curious.

"What have you got there?"

"It's a letter from my daughter, Mandy. Want to hear it?"

"Is it long? The pub's just around the corner."

"No, she's only eight. It's just a few sentences. Listen, 'Dear dad, I hopp (she's spelt it H-O-double-P) you are coming back. I love you. Please send me a letter. Love, Amanda.'"

"Jesus, that's tough."

"What are the chances?"

"Of what?"

"Of me coming back."

"Oh. Well, not that bad really. Conspiracy is a hard charge to prove. If all you boys can only stick together you might just do it, but it's important that you get one thing straight. The cops will be trying to split you up so that one of you turns in the rest. If you're guilty, that is!"

We smiled in the mirror.

"So the important thing is trust. You're going to have to trust each other and stay solid. No deals, otherwise you might have serious problems."

And that's right. The time to get worried would be when one of us got paranoid about serving time and did a deal for a light sentence. But even then there's not much point in getting upset about that sort of thing, or taking it personally if it happens. When you deal with rogues and play the con you learn to take the bad with the good, otherwise you shouldn't be in it. If something goes wrong, or you find you've been played for a sucker, or ripped off by people you trusted, you must remember that that's exactly what you were trying to pull on someone else. If you get upset, it eats away at you inside and your whole life turns into an angry, destructive process. That's another thing I learned early on, the hard way, in the orchards near Mildura where I had landed on a whim because the train ride was free.

At that time, fruit growers paid transport to bring their seasonal pickers up from Melbourne and while I had no intention of working, I was happy to accept the lift. I had just been sacked from the circus, was out for a holiday, and on the lookout for the opportunity to pull my first full-scale con!

"Make your booking here for Ma's boarding!" A ratty little bloke was pushing through the crowded carriage brandishing a clipboard. "Brand new, centrally located, five bucks a day, private room, bed, breakfast and dinner! Transport to the fields laid on. Fillin' fast!"

There was a storm of questions from the pickers. Where? Who? Since when? It was an extra good deal, sounded much better than the hessian digs the growers supplied, and the agent was writing names frantically.

"Two days in advance to secure the bookin'. Thanks, folks. Just present yer receipts at Ma's!"

A flurry of cash changed hands, and then I found myself the subject of the little man's beady gaze.

"What about you, sir? You look like you could use some ol'-fashioned home cookin'!"

"No, bugger that! What I could use is a drink! I'm staying at the pub!"

His name was Eddie and when he had finished his rounds he returned to my carriage, wormed his way into a tiny space next to me, and struck up a cheerful conversation. It turned out he been a "hitinerant" for years and knew the game inside out, including all the scams, rorts, schemes, and cons awaiting the unwary picker. I confided that I was in the same business and it would take a game bird to catch me, and he smiled knowingly, suggesting there might be a dollar or two in a quick partnership of convenience.

"There's ten thousand hitinerants movin' in," he growled, "and it's survival of the fittest!"

We chatted conspiratorially about schemes and scams for a while and as he seemed to know what he was talking about, I could imagine what pitfalls awaited the boarders at Ma's. And it made good sense to join forces with someone who knew the scene.

"All right, I'm in. What sort of stuff are you talking about?"

"Well, I'll tell you somethin', Hayden," he whispered. "There's no such thing as Ma's Boardin'. That sort o' stuff."

I roared laughing and Eddie joined in and the more the poor innocent pickers stared at us, the more we laughed.

Apparently some friend of my new partner was going to pick us up, but when we pulled up at the station and everyone else had bolted for the pub, we were alone on the platform. Eddie was eyeing off a public pool just over the road and, seeing it was hot as hell, he suggested that while we were waiting for his friend we might have a swim.

"But we'll have to take turns because ya can't leave yer stuff just lyin' around like in Kiwiland, Hayden!" He giggled. "Too many like us around." I was boiling, so I jumped at the chance to go first, grabbing two dollars from my wallet, and stripping down to shorts.

"Be cool, Hayden!" Eddie joked, and I dismissed a sudden uneasy feeling.

When the sticky, over-warm, over-chlorinated water had washed away the worst of the heat I returned to the station, dripping pool water and fresh sweat onto a deserted platform. No Eddie, no suitcase. The place was empty except for an old, wearied stationmaster.

"There's ten thousand itinerants moving in," he said, "and if you ask me, you haven't got half a dog's chance of finding your mate, or your suitcase."

"Bad odds," I said.

"They'd steal the shirt off your back," he said, straight-faced.

I had no money, no clothes, no shoes—not even a booking at Ma's. I worked in the fields and slept in a hessian bunk for three days in shorts. My feet hurt. I was mosquito-bitten, sunburned, itchy, angry, hungry, and had learned to hate grapes. But when I finally picked up a cheque—enough to buy clothes and a decent bed and a solid binge—I found the humour to laugh, and hitched a ride out of town with three young Greeks in an old Valiant sedan.

They told me they had jobs organised at a fruit cannery about sixty miles over the border in South Australia, with proper hostel lodgings and good casual money. We got on pretty well from the start, slugging from a bottle of Greek booze and laughing about my mate Eddie, but they were intense lads and I hesitated over their offer to team up. I decided firmly against it when, at the border, the cop pulled back the hammer of his pistol and ordered us out of the car.

"None of you bastards move," he said, the four of us in line against the car, our arms and legs stretched out, American-style.

"I just hitched a lift!" I squealed, and the Greek next to me spat at the ground. They were armed robbery boys, vicious bastards the three of them—the four of us, according to the cops.

The hours I spent standing under guard, sweltering in the sun while the police checked my identity, turned out to be instructive. It was obvious that my three friends wouldn't be needing their employment, and if the police thought I was dark enough to be a Greek, so might the cannery. And so it did, as easy as the circus.

"And you are . . .?" the employment officer asked.

"Spiros. Spiros Cosmos."

"Well, Cosmos, you'll be with the unloading detail. Six till four. Room thirty in the Greek wing."

The cannery workers were segregated according to race and I was to room with the dirtiest animal I have ever met. He was coated in weeping pimples, never bathed or washed his clothes, played with himself until he was silly, and I was stuck with him.

"For God's sake, George! Do you have to do that where I can see you?"

"Whassamatter, Greek boy?"

"Well, at least you could wash! The whole room stinks!"

In time I made good friends with the others and we had a ball together, but this bloke was a woeful exception and straight away I had to start plotting his departure.

But first he nearly got rid of me because he spoke broken English badly, and I was supposed to interpret. I tore down to the library to bone up on the Greek alphabet but that wasn't good enough when the foreman asked me to speak the native lingo.

"Listen, Spiros. Can you tell your mate not to put the labels on upside down? I can't seem to get it through his thick skull."

"Sure, boss," I said, but neither could I, and neither could anyone.

When he continued putting labels on the wrong way up, I was carpeted and called on to explain.

"Sorry, boss, it's nothing to do with the language. He's thick. You'll have to sack him."

But no such luck. There was a labour shortage and they just shifted him down to where the rest of us were unloading sugar from the trains. It spoiled an enjoyable job, because the other Greeks had caught on to my act quick smart and reckoned it was a great joke. They gave me language lessons and called me foreman, and took orders — all of them, except for my room-mate. He was a lazy bugger, even by my standards, and in my capacity as foreman I thought I should have the power to boot him good and hard in the arse, but the others refused to back me up against another Greek. So when the trains came in he shifted one hundredweight bag, reckoned that was his quota, and dropped off to sleep while we sweated by. He slumbered in squalid luxury until at last a simple but magnificent plan took shape. I worked his countrymen so hard that they began to complain bitterly, and every time they complained I pointed to their mate sound asleep on a sugar bag.

Three days of it was enough to break their spirit. We waited until we had unloaded our quota and George was snoring among the produce left on the train. Softly, softly, we built a wall of sugar bags around him, right up to the carriage roof. We built it so thick there was no way he could possibly shift it. And when the train started up to move on to its next destination and we heard muffled shouts for help we bade a solemn farewell to George "the filthy", on his lonely way to canneries unknown!

"That'll make the bastard work," I shouted, as the train wheezed off into the distance.

We had some pretty good times together, those Greeks and I.

For a start, a thousand girls lived in a hostel a hundred yards away, strictly off limits, but that was merely a pleasant kind of challenge. It simply meant we had to find other forums for our mutual amusement, and as they were as desperate for mixed company as we were, any old forum would do. Even an old abandoned Holden with the engine missing attracted a posse of females large enough to push us to the drive-in movies. They bought the tickets, we bought chicken and champagne, and we all crammed inside in shifts. Then after all the food and booze and groping everyone could stand, we walked home.

"Keys are in the glovebox, mate," I said to the attendant as we sauntered past. "She's all yours."

When the season drew to a close we were laid off but I had learned lessons valuable for the con. I could easily pass myself off as a Greek, a Spaniard, a Yugoslav or an Italian, and that was a great help in avoiding cops. Some time later, for example, when the police were hot on my tail over a pub brawl, I was approached by two uniformed blokes in a bar.

"You're Hayden Haitana, aren't you," one said. "We've got a warrant for your arrest."

"Sorry mate, wrong guy."

"You're a Kiwi, aren't you?"

"Definitely not. I'm Spanish descent."

"What's your name?"

"Adrian Santana. Sounds like Haitana but I can assure you I'm Spanish. You ask my mate, Pete, here."

My friend Pete, whose story I'll come to shortly, agreed that I was Adrian Santana, but they were cleverer than that. Cynically, they told me to say something in Spanish. I raised my face contemptuously and spat out (getting it completely wrong):

"Dos hombres no comprende Español."

Pete, who was an interpreter by profession and knew what I meant, turned to them and "translated".

"You two bastards don't speak Spanish," he said, and our friends were apologetic.

"Yeah, all right. Fair enough. Our mistake."

Chapter Eight
MURPHY AND PETE

I was flat busted broke when I left the cannery so my new lodgings were nothing fancy, a sheet of corrugated iron in Port Adelaide. And there, destitute and demoralised, I fluked on the greatest lurk of all time — the Painters and Dockers. I heard about a "casual corner" where anyone who wanted a wharf job gathered in the mornings, and once you were known you were pretty well guaranteed a day's work. After a while, I graduated to the permanent job of security officer (would you believe it?) and under my regime I believe the phrase "knocking off from work" took on a whole new meaning. Despite my originally good intentions, the Painters and Dockers were a resourceful bunch and they could get anything past me — all kinds of high quality merchandise which had "fallen off the back" of ships.

When at last I saw the futility of trying to stop this pilfering it was only right and proper that I should get in on the act, and it was then I learned the glorious meaning of the word status. It means everybody is desperate for something you've got, and in my case, the dockers wanted nothing more than occasional attacks of blindness. It didn't go unnoticed either. The management was on my back in a big way.

"Come on, Haitana. You're not searching the workers properly and you know it. They're all bloody thieves so look in their lunch boxes, for God's sake!"

"Righto, boss!" I'd smile, and I followed my new instructions to the letter. But it did nothing to stop the problem. In fact it got worse.

"Hello, Hayden!" a cheery docker would shout as he neared the checkpoint, struggling under the weight of a crate.

"Gidday, Bruce. Watcha got there?"

"Jesus, mate, don't ask me to put it down. It's a portable welder. Weighs a bloody ton!"

"No, that's all right. Just give us a look in your lunch box."

"What?"

"I've gotta check your lunch box to make sure you're not pinching stuff. Okay?"

"Oh . . . orright. But hurry, will ya? You be at the pub tonight, Hayden? Can ya do with some glasses?"

"Yeah. Probably do with a few."

I have never seen so many rules broken—there were no rules. If you wanted something done it could be done. It was great fun working there and we even did a bit of horse training, Painters and Dockers style. If a local bloke was having trouble getting his animal to swim we had the solution. We'd get him to bring it down to the docks in a float, unload it for him, walk it to the edge of the wharf and heave it into the port river. Half the poor buggers were expecting us to lower the horse down by crane or something and business dried up after word got around. But it worked! At this time I was using my contacts in New Zealand to supply racehorses through the port to anyone who wanted them, but my interest in racing as a whole, still tarnished by those teenage experiences, was confined to the occasional punt.

In my position as gatekeeper I enjoyed sudden waterfront popularity but I honestly shudder to think what came through that gate. Though I lived in fine style with the best of everything, when word went around the docks of an upcoming "operation" it used to scare the hell out of me. "Them that asks no question . . ." was the rule of thumb, and it was sometimes heavily enforced.

For a year or so I was able to stay ignorant of more sinister goings on, but after one particular shipment came through there was a series of bashings and all kinds of threats floating around, so I figured it might be drugs. I just suspected it. I never knew for sure, but it looked to me like a top time to get out.

Nevertheless, the experience had been invaluable, watching the masters at work without being totally involved, and I felt far more confident about the con. The problem was that after dealing with the dockers for so long I was anxious to find a more aboveboard kind of work for a while—good honest toil among good honest men—and I was told the South Australian steel city of Whyalla offered a hard worker the best prospects. It was great advice because I ended up spending a few years there and having a top time of it too. I have terrific memories of Whyalla and it is a terrible shame that I can't ever, ever go back.

Again, finding work was easy. I applied for a job as site manager of an exploration set up and on the understanding I had secured the position I hitched a ride with a truckie heading out there. Given my total lack of experience it should, perhaps, have seemed strange that I was going straight to the top, but it sounded fair enough to me and I was prepared to accept the responsibilities. I strode manfully into the manager's office to shake hands with Murphy, the person I was about to replace. He loathed and despised me at first glance.

"Site Manager! You want my fuckin' job, do you?" He glared. "You get your fuckin' arse out of here, sonny, and get to fuckin' work!"

Oww! My job, in fact, turned out to be the lowliest available, oiling a crushing plant, every hour on the hour through the nightshift. It was a lonely, crushing bloody bore, but despite this temporary setback I refused to let Murphy get on top of me.

It was so obviously illogical to spend eight hours performing a total of forty minutes' work that I welded up a reservoir which could hold an entire shift's worth of oil, then designed a feeder mechanism held in place by a piece of timber. When I came on shift I did the greasing, set up the oil feeder system, then stripped off my overalls to disco gear underneath and headed off to town for a rage. For months I partied all night and slept all day, but like all great dodges, it was much too good to last.

One night the piece of timber vibrated free and the feeder collapsed. Hours would have passed as oil burned away and the vibrations would have grown gradually stronger and stronger. I was at my usual disco haunt in town, telling some brunette about the flying snakes of Borneo and how much trouble they'd given my exploration team while I tried to sneak a look down her blouse. I remember it vividly because the barman spoiled my concentration with the message.

"Hayden, there's some bloke from the rig on the phone . . . urgent."

"Probably hit paydirt," I said to the brunette, but I wouldn't have sounded convincing. It would have sounded like I was in deep shit. That mate of mine Pete was on the blower and I started shaking, because as Murphy might put it, "the news was fuckin' grim".

"Hold onto your hat, mate," he warned, "because you're in big bloody trouble. The plant seized and everything came down and some bloke's been killed! If I were you I'd clear out!"

But you can't clear out after something like that, and I sped back to join the crew. Later, shreds of overall were being found among the overburden as all of us worked under the floodlights, chucking rocks and dirt everywhere, our arms and hands scratched and bleeding. In that light you could barely recognise anyone under their hard hats, and I was worried silly about bumping into Murphy.

I made every resolution under the sun that night, outrageous promises to the heavens, if only there could be some kind of mistake. I'd been living it up in town while some bloke, probably with a wife and kids, lay bleeding to death under a pile of rocks, and it was my fault. We worked on for hours until I finally gave it a rest and stumbled over to the cookhouse for a cup of tea.

The cook looked at me kind of strangely—in fact, very strangely. His mouth opened, and closed, and opened again.

"Haitana! What the . . .? You're supposed to be dead! Hey, are you all right? You look awful!"

"Shit!"

"Yeah. Shit, all right! You better go tell Murphy to call this off. He's up at the office with the cops."

"Murphy?"

It's fortunate I was in shock because otherwise I might well have fled, and it's lucky Murphy was just as deep in shock because he appeared genuinely glad to see me. He ranted on for a few minutes, then stopped abruptly and shook his head. As I started on a hurriedly concocted excuse he simply raised his hand, and pointed to the door. Nothing more was said about it but I found myself transferred to dayshift, condemned to good honest toil among good honest men.

Cons have a magnetic attraction for cons, and when word of Haitana's disco scam filtered through the camp, my friend Pete seemed to look at me in a new light. He was a curious cove: a tall, slim, chubby-faced Pommy, of very few words. He spent much of his time behind the closed door of his room, tinkering with a guitar, meditating and listening to The Shadows. You couldn't help feeling there was more to this solid, dry, sensible fellow than met the eye. He made a habit of dropping by my room early in the evening and we sat together drinking quietly for hours. And the next day he would thank me for a great night. Needless to say he wasn't an easy man to get to know, but I was content to let him take his time and after a month or so he finally broke the silence of our regular evening binge.

"You know what, Haitch?"

I looked up in surprise to find him gazing at me.

"What?"

"Never go to work the day after a day off."

I nodded gravely and we returned to our contemplation, but I heard a slight whimper and Pete's shoulders started to shake and his face went red and moments later both of us were pounding the aluminium walls of the room, in hopeless hysterics.

"What do you think about teaming up?" he said when we recovered, his face alive with an intense enthusiasm.

"What to do? I mean, yes! But what?"

"Well, I have one or two enterprises on the side. Look, put it like this. I've got four or five languages, right? And you look like you could be foreign, right?"

The conversation continued into the night, covering issues like marketing and migrants and image, and the motor and whitegoods trades; by dawn the partnership was cemented and we were officially in business. The camps were full of migrants and they formed a powerful segment of the Whyalla market, but they were highly suspicious of the white Australian retailers. Our business was to become middlemen between the two, and it took off from day one. For example, if a Yugoslav wanted a washing machine he would give us the money to buy it on his behalf so he wouldn't be ripped off. We then purchased some second-hand bomb, or at best an inferior model, and kept the difference. It worked from the retail angle as well because we demanded commissions from our suppliers. The money rolled in.

There were risks involved and I had to exercise a little muscle on the occasions when our merchandise blew up, but the migrants knew full well we were taking a cut for our trouble and respected our right to make a profit. They figured it was better value to use us than the regular businessmen because at least they knew who to come and thump if they felt they had been conned. Make-goods took only a small percentage of our overall earnings.

Second-hand car sales were among the most rewarding. I knew this fellow whose uncle owned a caryard out on the highway, and he had mentioned that I might get a good deal if I said I was studying at university because the old chap liked people to further their education. I chose the cheapest car on the lot, a clapped out Mark One Zephyr, at a hundred and fifty dollars. I offered fifty down and another fifty when the money came through for my university books.

"Really? What course are you studying?" the old fellow asked, and I had to think for a moment because he was a sincere old bugger and I didn't like to tell a bare-faced lie.

"Law," I said with a good measure of truth, and he dropped the price to fifty dollars, no rego.

Of course I had it on the market straight away, trying to convince a Yugoslav mate of mine that it was worth four hundred.

"No. I want one yellow, sports, two door, fast. I want yellow and I not pay four hundred for this one."

Easily fixed! I punched a few holes in the muffler, welded up the back doors, knocked the handles off and coated it in yellow plastic paint. Within a few hours I had it back to my mate and as he struggled with his decision, I started it up and trod down hard on the accelerator. The old warhorse roared through its holed exhaust.

"Fast," he agreed, and forked out the money then and there. He got two trips to town out of it before he was pulled up by the cops. Usually you get nightmares about running into people you've conned like that because they might want to kill you, but my Yugoslav friend was an exception. I came upon the poor bugger in a bar about two years later and he chastised me gently.

"Hayden? You one shit of car salesman."

In fact the migrants were surprisingly tolerant of us, partly because we specialised in making terrible fools of Australians who showed any hint of racial prejudice—a deliberate marketing tactic which we stumbled on by accident.

I was dark to begin with, and usually even darker with dust from the coke ovens, and one evening at the pub Pete started grinning over an idea he had to stir up some trouble. A violent argument was brewing between some Australians and white South Africans about which race was treated worse—the Aborigines or the South African blacks. At exactly the right moment, when they were about to come to blows, Pete breasted the bar right next to them.

"I'll have a pint of beer and a glass of water for the black bastard in the corner," he said, and the conversation stopped. Pete turned to the table.

"Seems a shame giving a clean glass to a nigger, doesn't it?"

The pub was silent and the air electric as he walked over to me and put the glass down.

"Thank you, Massah. Most generous, Massah."

And like lightning one of the South Africans charged over and swiped the glass from my hand.

"Stand up for yourself!" he shouted. "You're every bit as good as he is!"

"No, boss," I said. "He pay my fare out here. He very good Massah!"

"Bloody oath!" thundered Pete. "He's my investment! I paid for him and I'm keeping him!"

That stirred them. The South African grabbed Pete, held him at knuckle-point and flung him out the door. As he vanished, I shouted after him.

"Hey, Massah! What about my pie?"

"What?" yelled the outraged South African. "Doesn't he feed you? We'll call the cops and have him up for slavery!"

Pete's voice drifted in from the footpath. "You keep him! He's not worth a bloody pie!"

What a night! Two counter teas, all the booze I could drink, and a long lecture from the South African on my rights as a human being. And it was good that he was doing all the talking because I had begun to slur, and I ran the risk of being pounded into the floor if my act slipped. When he started on the questions, it was time to call it off.

"You my Massah now, boss! I polish your shoes!" I whined. Disgusted that his hours of argument and walletful of conscience had got nowhere, my new owner stamped out.

You can't con an entire town indefinitely, but we did pretty well. I worked in Whyalla four times under four different names, living it up too, until Pete and I burned our bridges with the sale of a clapped out, sixty dollar, second-hand Austin I had bought for the short run into town.

When the big rains came, those fifty miles might as well have been fifty thousand. It was impossible even for a four-wheel drive to get through, and camp became a boring, soggy mess. We workers had nothing to do but get dirty and drunk. One day, thoroughly shot, Pete and I decided that whatever it took, we were going into town. All we needed for the passage was an army duck. The Austin looked like a likely candidate for conversion, and it was easier than it sounds. We waterproofed the electrics, the floor and doors, ran snorkels up for the carby and exhaust, loaded three cases of beer, and were ready to be cheered off by our sadly duckless mates.

"You'll never make it!" they laughed after us. "The road's turned into the bloody river!"

We made it all right but the journey took two days, and we hadn't had a drink for twenty-four thirsty hours by the time we hit town. The hotels were jammed with stranded mine workers unable to get back to work and toey as buggery because they were being docked pay. We were heroes for having made the run and it was soon obvious why, with half the town trying to book the back seat for our return passage. We could have made a fortune out of running a ferry service but, flushed with success and ready for a skinful, we didn't want to know about anything but booze.

Pete and I had split up when the first offers came in, some Italian bidding "sixty bucks for the duck". I shook my head but then someone else raised, and so on. I'd have been a mug not to sell at three hundred.

That's where it should have stopped, but by now the word of our feat was out all over town and the mood was ugly. If we didn't want to use the duck, sell up or else. At the next pub they held another auction and I sold it again, and then once more for luck, cash on the nail, delivery in one hour. When I caught up with Pete, he was breathless.

"Guess what?"

"You sold the car?"

"Yeah." He sounded surprised. "But twice! Two fifty and two seventy five. We gotta get out of here!"

"Me, too. That makes five buyers and over thirteen hundred bucks, and you're right, we better clear out fast."

We hitched a road train east, never to return, but we heard later that the consequences were enormous. We should have taken the duck with us because there was a violent bust-up over which of the buyers owned it. It broke out in the bar of this hotel and we were told it was very bloody rough. In the end a couple of Yugoslav blokes ganged up together and creamed the rest. After that there was a virtual death warrant out for us in the fair city of Whyalla. Even among our faithful migrants the welcome was worn out.

This was when Hayden Haitana became Adrian Santana. I forget what Pete called himself. We conned and boozed and womanised our way through the eastern states. We became exceptionally cunning at getting jobs, developing techniques which became standard practice. The night before an interview I'd hop off to the library and study up on whatever skill was required. With a little extra manoeuvring, I wound up by this method in some quite responsible positions.

But my employment was never long-term because while I could get away with knowing nil about the job, I couldn't help taking advantage of situations which cried out for fraud. I was never actually caught with my fingers in the till but only because I had developed the sixth sense essential to the con: that's the sense of knowing when, and when not, to run like a dog!

Chapter Nine
SANTANA

Free beer! The advertisement marked "Brewery Plant Operator" looked like heaven and I was instantly desperate for the job. I got straight on the telephone, speaking to a fellow named MacPherson, and after I rambled on about my long experience with New Zealand breweries he asked me to come in for a chat when his shift started the following day. I was hopelessly unqualified for the job but the plan was simply to front early and use this fellow's name as a fake reference. Twenty minutes before his shift I wandered in, asking to speak to my old mate Mac about the supervisor's job. Of course, as I was a mate of Mac's they had to put me onto one of the other managers, whom I earbashed mercilessly about our longstanding friendship.

"Well, if you're a friend of Mac's, I'd say you've got the job, no worries!" he said, "and here he is now . . . you might want to have a word with him about it, eh?"

I strode over to "Mac", full of confidence, but I kept my voice pretty low.

"Mr MacPherson? Hayden Haitana. They just put me on as the new supervisor, but all my experience is in New Zealand breweries so they reckon you'll teach me how you do things over here."

It was a walkover. I soon learned the trade well enough to survive, and Mac and I became old mates anyway.

After a while, however, it became necessary to move on. Pete and I became steadily bolder, always on the lookout for a more lucrative opportunity, and when the Victorian Railways advertised for track workers it looked like a big one. The difficulty was that I had a weak left eye and would probably fail the medical, but we were hardly going to let that stop us. By comparison to the other stunts we'd been pulling, it was easy enough to fix.

Pete went in first, memorised the bottom line, and recited it to me a few times out in the waiting room. When the time came to test my weak eye, I read the big letters off the top of the chart, then paused, feigning impatience.

"Look, let's save all this crap and I'll just read the bottom line, okay?" And before he could interrupt, I parroted away and got it perfect.

"That's very good," said the doctor. "Not many people can read that line from here."

"Well, my right eye's good, but my left is even better," I confessed. Hayden Haitana was working on the railroads!

We were laying track on a new route from Sydney to Broken Hill with a gang of Yugoslav migrants, and in some ways it was much like the fruit cannery. As none of them spoke much English they gained the impression that I was their foreman, and followed my orders while Pete and I took it easy. Then when one of the proper bosses came along he was so impressed with the way I had things running I was offered a promotion.

"What did you get?" asked Pete anxiously as I returned home with a dozen beer and a king-sized smile.

"Who is responsible for 'Allocation of overtime and accurate recording of hours worked into official logs'?" I beamed.

Pete's eyes widened as far as his mouth did. "Shit! Surely not you?"

"It's the big one! Timekeeper!"

We whooped and danced a jig in the kitchen. Heaven stared us in the face. Within days I had organised it so that everyone was working four hours a day while I was putting ten hours in the book. Our Yugoslav labourers were delighted and fully understood that we should take a generous cut of their additional wages. Under the Haitana regime the railroads were paradise and they even called me boss.

"You bloody good boss, Hayden!" a grateful worker would say as he rested in the shade of a tree guzzling beer bought with overtime. And how could there be any argument?

Our standard wage was about eighty dollars a week but the overtime concession lifted me to well over four hundred and in those days that was airline pilot territory. There were other top lurks too.

I operated a spare parts racket, selling the migrants cheap gear for their cars, a wonderfully simple fraud. If they needed new brakes, so did the Government ute, but that ute needed so many distributors and exhausts and rebores that eventually some administration sharpie called me on the telephone to check up. After taking a moment to gather my composure, I put on my most disgusted voice.

"It's a bloody lemon, all right! And you should get into those spare parts people for the rubbish they keep fitting it with! When are we going to scrap this pile of shit and get a new ute?"

It was a good stalling tactic but that sixth sense was buzzing. Pete and I knew the whole scheme had to come crashing sometime soon. We cleared out to Adelaide. It was lucky that we did, because a series of disasters occurred the following week. One of the Yugoslavs got blind drunk on duty and smashed his hand up; some of the others had an accident with a taxi in the company ute, just after leaving the pub in town on work time; and a freight train was delayed hours because my gang had knocked off early without replacing a section of track. All of us got the sack, Pete and I in our absence of course, but the railways had been too good to us and I wasn't ready to give up on it yet.

And so it went on for some time. If I was sacked on the Friday I would be hired on the Monday, under a different name and in another part of the state. I had six different jobs under six different names over a period of a few years. It was such an easy con I was able to get about twenty-five of my tame migrants into work by filling in their applications and doing their tests and medicals. All I asked in return was a small cut of their wages.

The hazard was that I had a hard time keeping track of who I was supposed to be, and I was close to coming unstuck when, on several occasions, I forgot altogether. In Sydney it created difficulty in the rail worker pubs: I was known as Bruce in one, David in another across the road, and Adrian up the street. That meant that when the patrons of each occasionally mixed, I could be called several different names in the one conversation.

I did suffer a kind of poetic justice for these railroad sins. It was about this time my jockey brother, "Pat the Rat" Haitana, arrived in Melbourne with a couple of Kiwi horses; one of them called Ah Jay was a dead-set champion. The trick was that no one in Australia knew anything about its form so the odds would be good. I'd gone down to Melbourne, and we were rubbing our hands, organising to punt the bum off its first run. I thought we'd get even better odds in New South Wales and as there were a few hundred dollars' railroad back pay supposed to be waiting for me there, I hopped the train back to Sydney for the punt. I was going to be rich!

On the eve of the big race I fronted at the rail office to pick up the money owing to me, only to find the cheque had been shipped off to where we were working out the back of beyond. They couldn't retrieve it until the following week and no amount of desperate pleading would bend the rules. So when Ah Jay romped home at sixteen to one, I barely had a cracker on it.

After that the horse was taken out of Pat's hands. It continued to do well and I think it might still hold several track records in the bush.

We had stood to make a profit of three thousand dollars with bugger all effort, and what went wrong was one of those simple, unforseeable balls ups. But we weren't going to be ruffled by one isolated disaster. The punt had to be the way to go. From then on gambling was my unshakeable passion. I still envy those who can go to the track with twenty dollars and have a great time losing it, just like I envy people who can have one drink, or smoke one cigarette.

And there's another side. Gambling—or rather losing—is the simplest way to get trapped into criminal schemes right across the board, whether you gamble with a business or on a horse. I know more people who have gone bad to pay for a failed gamble, than have taken up the life of con by choice. The courts and newspapers are full of it—from blue collar punters to company directors—they start losing, then lose worse to get even. And if addicted gamblers can't win fair and square they'll bend the rules or break them to stack the odds on their side. I was gambling, losing, and breaking the rules long before I met up with the horse called Fine Cotton.

Chapter Ten
BAINSEY

Curiously enough, the big storm for which my career was headed was preceded by a lull, a period of stability and respectability which overshadowed even the punt. I still gambled most of my money, but it was money earned fair and square from a good job which I won on my own merit.

One of the big oil companies was advertising for candidates to take a refinery steam cracking course. I had always been interested in chemical things so I wrote them a letter. I was flabbergasted when they replied, requesting that I report for a series of examinations which continued for six weeks until they had narrowed the field to only a dozen applicants, and I was one! I swotted up on hydrocarbons and petrochemicals and molecular structure, and while I didn't understand much of it, I kept going until I could quote the information off pat and had the job. The oil company enrolled me in a twelve-month advanced course which I passed quite well, and I thought my career—my whole damn life—was set.

And then I met her, a gorgeous, willowy creature who swept me off my feet. We dined and danced and fell in love, and moved in together, and the talk was all of marriage. As it happened, there were several small matters in which she had not been entirely honest. First, she was already married. Second, she had the temper of a shrew. And third, she was a nymphomaniac. These three things, in isolation, can sometimes be dealt with but together they make one hell of a package. There were scenes of chaos in discos as I fought off rival males, scenes of embarrassment in restaurants as she flew off the handle, and scenes of terror in our bedroom as she described the size and nasty disposition of her husband, who was "not exactly separated" but "just away for a while".

When he came home one night, I fully expected to be killed. He was huge, and tough, but he seemed to have been through the whole thing before. In a tired voice he wished me luck.

It was too much. The next day I astounded the careers officer by asking for a transfer to an offshore oil rig. The best he could do was something out in the middle of the Simpson desert working for an altogether different oil company, but that suited me fine. I loved oil — I could just about drink the stuff — but, as I was soon to discover out in the middle of the Simpson Desert, my new company was looking for gas. And then the exploration money ran out and the team was disbanded. There were no vacancies back at my old company, and once again I found myself on the trail of an easy dollar. Port Adelaide here I come!

I returned to the docks and earned my ticket as a customs clerk, met Monica, and a year later we were married. I had sown more than my fair share of wild oats and honestly believed I was ready to settle down, raise a family, and do all the things that normal people do. But the one thing I hadn't fully reckoned on was Haitana's law: "Don't count your chickens, because the eggs are off." The recession came, and I was retrenched when the whole customs scene tightened up. The retailers had been screaming about all the stuff they were losing in transit, and while I was never convicted of any associated crime, I must admit that my old attacks of blindness were recurring, along with a counting problem. If a hundred transistors came in I could only count eighty, if a dozen bottles of booze came in I could only count ten.

I was out of work and on welfare, punting away all the money I had saved from my oil job. Then we sold our house to raise more, and the horses took that and then all our money was gone. It was the moment every gambler dreads, when you don't even have enough left to take a chance.

I was shaken and desperate. There was no money for milk, no money for bread, no money for beer. Then, along came Bainsey.

Bainsey ran a rough waterfront pub which I used to frequent down at Port Adelaide, and from our first meeting I could tell he was a bigger rogue than most. At one stage he had been a major punter in Melbourne, but that had got the better of him and he moved to Port Adelaide rather than risk broken knees. He knew what it was to be down on your luck and when I told him of my awful bind, straight away he proposed a loose deal which was to have frightening consequences. He floated me enough to get by and took me into a partnership based wholly on "untoward opportunity" — the con.

"Hayden Haitana," he said as I nodded my agreement, "never let a small setback put you off! You and me are going to take this little port by the short and curlies and tip it on its rear!"

"All right!" I enthused, my faith restored. "Bloody ripper, Bainsey!"

A ripper! You only had to ask the thousands of Port Adelaide layabouts he ripped off! It still baffles me how we survived those years of razor's edge living, but I'm pretty sure it had to be fools' luck.

Bainsey was a short, beefy man with blonde curls and a maniac's energy, and not what you'd call a modest gambler. In fact he was the maddest punter I've ever met and what's more, it didn't matter a damn where the stake came from or how he got hold of it.

"The pub's got money, hasn't it? We'll raid the till and pay it back!"

"Fair enough. But what happens when we lose it?"

Bainsey would look at me like I was crazy. "Lose it? We'll just sell a few kegs and back something better!"

Our lives quickly developed into a continuous battle of wits with the area's S.P. bookmakers, the owners of the pub and the brewery which supplied us. Everyone we dealt with copped a terrible caning. On occasions we came fairly close to it ourselves: one day I walked into the bottle shop to find Bainsey well on the way to being strangled to death by a couple of heavies. Just in time, a tame cop happened by.

"Everything all right, Bainsey?" he asked, eyeing off the opposition.

"Sure, sure," gasped Bainsey, straightening his tie. "The boys were just leaving."

The heavies had arrived on behalf of a local S.P. bookie, who was fed up with our style of punt — everything on credit. At one stage we were thirty thousand dollars in the red to this bloke, and completely broke. We checked the pub but we'd already spent the full payroll. There was nothing left in the till.

A day passed tensely, without inspiration, and Bainsey and I found ourselves together at a Sunday barbecue shaking like derelicts.

"Tell you one thing, Haitch," he moaned, "we just might be in for an attack of the slows."

"What's slows?"

"It's when a bullet catches up with you."

Neither of us could raise a smile. We stared glumly into our beers.

"Surprised you two clowns aren't at the track," said a local loud-shirt.

"Nothing doing at the track, smartarse," snarled Bainsey.

"There is down at Victor Harbour — Sunday trots."

Bainsey and I stared at him and he backed away. We turned to each other for an instant, then dashed for a newspaper and telephone.

"Listen, Hayden, these guys are going to do us over whether we owe them thirty thousand or three hundred thousand, so we might as well go for it."

Bainsey was crouched over the racing pages, chewing on the end of a pen and breathing heavily through his nose.

"Might as well," I agreed, my ears burning.

Minutes later we were on the blower to the same bookie we were badly in debt to.

"Ten thousand on Pacific Flyer!" I heard Bainsey say, and the adrenalin surged through me.

"Three to one. A cert!" he told me and slapped me on the back, his eyes ablaze, grinning like our problems were over.

Pacific Flyer or whatever it was went down badly and that meant we owed forty thousand, but it was feeling like play money and as the meet progressed our tally got worse and worse.

"Listen to me. Now, you listen. You bastards had better be able to settle," hissed the bookie down the line. "I don't go in much for this doubling up bit."

But that was our only chance, to keep doubling until something came home.

We owed nearly a hundred and twenty thousand by the time our ship came in, a long shot in the last race at about fourteen to one, and the only bet which could have saved us. We hugged each other, went out for tea and got blind, and over the closing beers we decided we never need fear the punt again. All we had to do was double up on credit! On Monday the bookies' runners arrived to give us the change—five hundred bucks—but that had to go straight to the brewery to cover raids on the hotel till.

That pub was the strangest business. No one was guaranteed wages because the whole payroll was usually riding on a horse, and so was the money we needed to buy stock, and so was every dollar we could con out of the patrons. Bainsey and I spent more time at the track than running the hotel.

Our records of accounts were non-existent and we once found ourselves in such a bad fix that Bainsey had to have an affair with a barmaid so she would raise a personal loan to cover the current deficit. Even she finally balked one night when we asked her to work overtime—we were about to bet the next payroll on a cert.

"You're sick! Both of you!" she screamed and went home.

We had a problem because we were sure the horse we planned to put the payroll on would get us out of another financial jam. We didn't want to spook the bookies with a single massive bet and that meant Bainsey and I had to hit them on course, in relays, just before the event. But we could hardly leave the pub unattended, and we were scratching our heads and pacing the bar when Bainsey decided to do the next worst thing.

"Banjo! Over here!" he ordered.

Banjo was a track rider and a hopeless alcoholic, the most unreliable member of our personal stable.

"Now, look. Hayden and I have got to get out to the track, so you're in charge. Close the doors at seven and no free drinks right?"

I went white. "Bloody hell, Bainsey!"

"No, you'll be right, won't you Banjo? What can happen in two hours?"

When we returned at 11 p.m. the place was the biggest show in town, packed out, everyone guzzling away at free drinks. It was down to the dregs of the spirits by then. All the beer, along with all the cigarettes and food, had gone.

"Where's the bastard we left in charge?" Bainsey shouted over the din.

"He's upstairs. Been up there with some tart since tea time."

We were in big, big trouble. No booze in the pub, no credit left with the brewery, the whole town knowing we were broke, and we'd used up a month's supplies in the first week. Bainsey's habit of flogging off kegs to private parties had reduced our stocks to minimum levels even before the great free binge. Ours was a pub with no beer — a pub with no bloody nothing.

"I can't believe it!" said Bainsey. "We've just chucked the biggest bash in the history of Port Adelaide and we weren't even here to see it!"

We should have been put in jail, but as usual Bainsey came up with a novel solution. We begged kegs from the other pubs, one at a time, rolling them down the main street by hand.

"If only we'd got that last leg!" I remember saying to my punting partner as we bumped and clattered along. "We'd be sitting pretty now!"

Bainsey shot me an ugly look. "That bloody Banjo is on his last leg! When I catch him he's fuckin' finished!"

It's a mystery how we kept the pub going until we had conned enough to buy stock, but the patrons were loyal and if we couldn't give them change for a while they didn't seem to mind. Bainsey and I had to work like dogs. If someone wanted a bourbon and coke we had to grab a glass and rush across the street to buy it at the neighbouring pub, where our plight was a great joke. Spirits drinking was actively discouraged, but when the time came to make up the menu boards for our counter lunches, it was another dash up the road to see what everyone else had to offer.

As the punt wouldn't seem to come to our rescue, and the S.P.'s had stopped credit on the doubling tactic, Bainsey and I had to arrive at other means of gradually restoring financial order.

Luckily the hotel was a sailors' haunt and the foreigners were generally regarded as fair game. They were good pigeons, with pockets full of cash from time at sea, and we swiftly established a series of brand new scams designed to relieve them of that burden. Vastly unfair punting practices and the local pool squad each took a fearsome toll. The pool table, especially, was the classic sting, and we reckoned that if our victims couldn't recognise an obvious set up when they saw it they deserved everything they got. We let them win for a while until the stakes rose high enough to make clobbering them worthwhile, then the standard of our team's performance suddenly, dramatically improved. It is hardly surprising that this resulted in some spectacular brawls, and we stung them badly on those, too.

Rather than disrupt trade, we tried to confine fighting to the back room, where there was only room for two opponents.

"Hey, hey, hey!" Bainsey bellowed when the situation reached flashpoint, "let's see some respect for the furniture around here!"

Next would come a suggestion that the sailors choose their champion and we ours, with side bets on the fight. Their choice was usually some seven foot bruiser with a nose flattened out like a pancake, and you should have seen their faces when we chose my jockey-sized brother, Pat. They hollered for anyone at all to cover their bets.

"A hundred says the scrawny bastard gets killed!" they shouted, and we all shook our heads and muttered.

"Two to one!"

But no takers.

"Three to one!"

We pounced. Pat was a martial arts expert, and fit from riding. He could be counted on to surprise the sailors. During one particularly fierce battle a drinker came into the bar to tell me Pat was out back, on the ground getting the stuffing punched out of him. I wandered off with a beer for a look. This sailor was kneeling on Pat's chest banging his head against the floor. I had a good laugh and returned to the bar to assure Pat's backers their money was safe.

"He's just waiting for the big bloke to get tired," I chuckled. Sure enough, in a few minutes my brother was out to announce he had given the sailor a walloping. We made a fortune out of these bar room scams and for a while the pub was in good financial shape. But then word of the cons got out on the waterfront in a big way and a local battle broke out.

It's not surprising that the waterfront hotels were getting a bad reputation. The opposition publicans were annoyed, and they began sending their bouncers over to teach us a lesson. Then we had to hire more bouncers, and so did they, until it got so heavy and the wages bill so high that we gave in, ended our scams and everyone called it off. This crying shame meant that Bainsey and I needed a replacement scheme fast.

It was a policeman friend of ours who put us onto it, and it was a beauty. For years it was his habit to meet incoming ships, making himself well-known to the senior officers and gradually winning their trust. As these friendships developed, he'd talk them into becoming part-owners of racehorses. In return for their contributions to training and stabling fees they were paid a percentage of the winnings, and were welcome to come out and see their animal anytime they were in port.

When they returned, usually in three months or so, our smiling policeman was there to greet them with a hefty bill and the news that the horse would need at least another three months' work to race. Of course no trainer ever went near the hack he trotted out for the seamen, and they might have bucked a little if they'd known they were in partnership with at least a hundred other suckers in the same mangy horse. It sounded fine to us, but it was a year before our version of the same con took shape, and in a far more complex form, as a service called "Haitana's Rent-a-horse".

Chapter Eleven
REAL CHAMOZZLE

"End of the line, Hayden," the solicitor said as the car pulled to a halt. I heard the hatchback clunk open. "Gillespie's supposed to be waiting in that blue station wagon parked over there."

I pushed the back seat forward for a better view, and there he was, the Phantom, already out of the wagon and striding toward us.

"What about the pub?"

"Just around the corner. That's where he's taking you."

"Good-o, then. Thanks for the lift."

I struggled out of the boot and then an arm was under mine. I turned, and John Gillespie looked at me. And I looked back into those pale blue eyes feeling a sudden rush of warmth. We'd have made a good team, the Phantom and me, if he'd listened. If he had listened, we'd be rich!

It's easy to be wise after the event, but I had lost count of the number of times I tried to convince him to drop the Fine Cotton ring-in and go with something else. I'd had a flawless change of plan, still with Fine Cotton, but involving far fewer people, far less expense, and absolutely no chance of detection. From before the Cotton plan went really bad until the day of the race, I was urging him to go with my own secret weapon, the "patent Haitana bomb". I had it ready, and the real Fine Cotton would have won that fourth event at Eagle Farm Racecourse on 18 August 1984, hands down, if only we'd used it.

The bomb was a chemical concoction I had used with success over a period of years. It dramatically boosted a racehorse's performance, and the beauty was it didn't show up in a swab. It was an almost perfect con, born, rather ironically, of a horse called Real Chamozzle. It came about like this.

It was a stifling summer Saturday afternoon. The Haitana clan was once again flat, punted-out and destitute, and even Bainsey had run out of inspiration. We were just scraping by on the dole, and in Port Adelaide that can get numbingly dull, especially on Saturday afternoon. Thank heaven I had heard about a stock sale happening, and for want of petrol money, rounded up Pat and my neighbour for the drive.

"But we haven't got any money!" complained my brother. "Why go to a stock sale if we can't bloody buy anything?"

"Because I was going nuts, that's why!" I snapped.

But if you're interested in racing, sales are always worth a look because you pick names to watch in the future. There was plenty of good blood there and Pat had his eye on a three year old called Real Chamozzle, which he thought had strong prospects and a long career ahead of it. We were interested to see how much he sold for. We positioned ourselves right up at the rails for the bidding, which was spirited and entertaining until this Real Chamozzle went under the hammer. For this horse there were no bids and I had to smile at Pat.

"Three hundred dollars!" shouted my neighbour, who was as broke as we were.

"Hell!" I whispered fiercely. "You know that bid is legally binding, don't you? You'll cop all sorts of strife if you can't pay."

"Four hundred!" came a voice from behind us and we sagged with relief.

"Four fifty!" thundered Pat beside me.

"Sold!" bellowed the auctioneer.

Pat turned around, a look of puzzlement on his face.

"Now, why did I do that?"

We found ourselves with just one afternoon to raise the money, and luckily chanced on a mad punter for whom Pat had ridden in the past.

"You should just see this beauty!" we glowed. "It's got to be worth a couple of grand but we bought cheap. We'll let you in on a half share for four fifty."

Our prospect hesitated for a few moments, because the name Real Chamozzle didn't inspire confidence, but eventually he was in and we were off the hook—better than that, because we were now half owners in a racehorse we hadn't paid a cent for. We couldn't believe our luck and that was very sensible, because it took a sharp turn for the worse shortly afterward.

I was picked up for drink-driving again and considering my record I decided not to answer the summons. At the same time Pat was at loggerheads with our copper friend, who had demanded that he honour a promise to ride for him. Pat refused, but the policeman was well aware of the outstanding warrant against me and was so annoyed he threatened to make my whereabouts known to headquarters unless Pat played ball. He was told to bite it because after all was said and done, we were friends with the copper, weren't we?

The next day I was in the slammer, Real Chamozzle went into the hands of another trainer, and Pat was out in the cold trying to raise my eight hundred dollar fine. They put me on a prison farm picking oranges, sunup to sundown; oranges, oranges, oranges. Oranges joined grapes on the list of pet hates. Oranges every bloody meal. It was brutal punishment and everyone on the farm was sick to death of bloody oranges. And wouldn't you know it? When Pat turned up to visit, all he brought me was a bag of bloody oranges. The other prisoners roared.

"Thanks, Pat," I said, remarkably composed.

"Let 'em laugh!" he whispered. "They're loaded with vodka."

For two months I picked oranges and still slurped happily on them with Pat when he arrived on regular visits. Obviously alcohol was outlawed on the farm, but he merely had to stop a few hundred metres up the road, grab an armful from a tree, inject the vodka with a syringe, and Bob's your uncle!

As it so happened I was using spare moments to design my own racing colours and Pat's loaded presents provided terrific inspiration. The colours, which years later would ride on a horse called Fine Cotton, were five oranges over gold.

Pat got hold of the fine money by selling our share of Real Chamozzle to our partner, the mad punter. It meant we lost all rights to the horse, which was a shame, but naturally we maintained a personal interest in his career: in fact we decided he owed us at least one win. The big temptation was to sneak the horse out of his new stables and race him somewhere ourselves. Naturally we gave in straight away.

As soon as I was freed from prison we checked up on coming events and decided Chamozzle was a good chance for a picnic meet the next weekend. Under cover of darkness we stole into his stables and stole out, not only with the horse, but with his trainer's colours and his float. And our confidence was well justified. Chamozzle left several horses at the barrier and streaked home to a win. We had a hundred on him at four to one and were ecstatic, until an official gently took me aside.

"You know that if we declare Real Chamozzle the winner he loses status as a maiden?" he said kindly. "Seems a shame to lose that at a picnic race for ten dollars and a sash."

The four hundred dollars in winnings didn't seem quite so bright when you looked at it that way. It wasn't our horse, the trainer would be bloody livid, and for sure the police would be called in.

"Tell you what I can do," the official said, "and that's call a restart because those other horses were too slow away from the barrier."

Shortly afterward Pat and I were heading back to the car for a can of beer, counting our blessings, when the process went into sudden subtraction. Chamozzle's real trainer was standing next to his own float, talking to his wife.

"Jesus, that looks just like my float," he said, as the horses came up for the restart. "What?" he shouted, looking straight at Chamozzle. "Those are my colours! And my horse!"

The consequences of Chamozzle winning a picnic event must have hit him hard. He looked shaken and we had no choice but to front him and do some fast talking, with an assurance that we'd instructed the jockey to pull the horse up in the re-run. And did that jockey have to pull! The horse was only beaten by half a length. Afterward the trainer was going to call the cops anyway. A quick call to our friend, the owner, with the suggestion that Chamozzle had badly needed a hit out, was all that saved our skins.

A year later, the horse had still failed to win a race. I told the owner he needed a new trainer. Me! He was so frustrated over the money he had paid out for no return he wasn't interested in campaigning any more, but I was sure Chamozzle had it in him to win. I offered to lease the horse for three years and business was done on the spot, but I couldn't take delivery until I made payment and I couldn't make payment until I ran into the local butcher.

He was waving a huge wad of notes around a local bar when I found him, and within a few hours both of us were drunk.

"All I want is the photo finish with my name on as owner for the wall of the shop," he repeated. "If you can do that you're a champion."

"All you gotta do is join me in the lease. You pay six weeks' training fees and you've got your photo. I personally guarantee it."

"Done!" he said, smacking the bar with his palm. "Let's have a whisky on it."

Real Chamozzle was a certain winner for one rock-hard reason. I was going to give him the bomb.

I had not been idle during the past twelve months. I was sure there must be a chemical compound which could boost a horse's performance and still not show up in current forms of swabbing, and I was determined to find it. First I studied all aspects of sports medicine, particularly methods used by foreign countries to boost athletic performance. Several were feasible for horses but everything I came up with was either too expensive, too dangerous for the animal, or too impractical in terms of getting it into the bloodstream. For example, there was one technique which involved draining an amount of blood to store for transfusion back into the body, after it had made up the shortfall and not long before the event. It allowed the heart to work at a slower rate to get the same amount of oxygen through the system. But while it improved performance the disadvantages were enormous. It was highly dangerous, and required complex equipment.

I consulted an academic I had known in New Zealand and his wife, for whom I had done favours over the years. Together we worked on a combination of substances and techniques which, on refinement, produced astounding results.

The problem we encountered was in obtaining the active chemical, because it had to be imported through a registered medical practitioner. However I did manage to establish a small source of supply. The difficulty my suppliers faced was to account for every gram of the stuff they used. As I needed ten grams per dose it might mean waiting three months while they shaved enough from their quota to make up one needle.

But it was worth the wait. The only elements which showed up in the swab were legal ones, which acted to block detection of the active substance.

The effect is not to make the horse run faster, but to enable it to maintain its performance over a much greater distance. Before I ever dared administer the compound to a horse I tried it out on my labrador, who dug up the entire back yard, then on myself (with unmentionable results) and then on a friend of mine who was suffering great distress from a broken left leg. The results were side-splitting. After a few hours he felt a little light-headed, then the pain went, and shortly afterward he was dancing on the table. It took some time to perfect the shot for racing, however, because the effects are not pronounced until some hours after administration and last only for a certain period, so if a race is delayed or is run well ahead of time there is no benefit whatsoever. And when it does take effect that horse had better be racing because he's a hell of a handful otherwise! It made for an awful drama at one particular country meeting.

I had given a horse his shot in the morning, and by the time we reached the track and had him in his stall he was rearing to go, highly aggressive and even more highly strung. Then they changed the whole race schedule. As I was about to saddle him up, a steward wandered over with the news that there was a wet section on the other side of the track, so all the sprint races had to be run first. Mine was entered in the mile and the delay could be hours.

"I want to race him now!" I protested. "He's all upset!"

"No. Sorry, mate. We can't possibly move the barriers until it dries up."

I took a look back at the horse and he was like a randy bull. He had already torn his rug to shreds and snapped one halter, and was now intent on savaging the neighbouring gelding. I couldn't possibly take him out for a walk because I would lose him for sure, so I jammed a thick piece of timber through the rail to restrict movement. He smashed it in ten seconds flat and he was getting worse. Another trainer and I strained on his head collar to hold him, and then a relay was set up: two people to hold him, two people to drink. By the time his race came, however, he was quiet as a mouse, and ran well back.

Gradually I refined the technique, found the proper doses and achieved success. Many an owner found himself suddenly delighted by a mediocre horse's vastly improved performance—then sadly disappointed by an immediate return to its original form.

I wasn't training the buggers, but I sure as hell was bombing them! The bomb also enabled me to fox around the odds because I could train one of my own horses to race over a mile and a half, then enter it for a sprint event. Its form for the sprint would be lousy because it was known as a stayer, so the odds were good, and even in a sprint the bomb made enough difference to virtually assure a win. The next start it would be entered over the longer distance and run to form. Bookies, punters and jockeys alike were highly confused by my unorthodox training techniques, but there was method in my madness.

Getting back to Real Chamozzle; with the bomb under him he walked it in, the strapper frantically waving towels at the home turn to keep him on the track, all of us on tenterhooks standing with our backs to the action. The photo finish which still hangs proudly on the butcher's wall shows him winning, with us in the foreground waving our winning tickets at the bookies.

With the "patent Haitana bomb" in my racing arsenal I should have been a millionaire by now, but bugger me if I ever seemed to have two coins to rub together when I needed something for the big punt. It was others who talked me into using up my supplies, and others who profited most. I went along for the ride, just like on the docks. I enjoyed the status of being the key part of other people's plans and the attention they showered on me, but in both situations, on the course and on the docks, I was a sucker. Money and houses and cars were promised and the promises were broken. Once the kind of people I was dealing with have the cash in their hands they're not willing to let go. There's nothing better than easy money, and at the same time, in many ways, there's nothing worse.

Chapter Twelve
APPRO

I was in search of good candidates for the bomb — hopeless horses with bad form and bad manners which I could pick up for almost nothing, because that's how much I had to spend. They still had to have some potential, however, and Appro was perfect for the part.

I had been in Melbourne to watch Pat ride, and the trainer he was working for was complaining bitterly about Appro's performance: eight starts for eight lasts.

"Temper like a madwoman," he spewed. "And I've got to give the mongrel a separate paddock or he won't let the other poor bastards eat. A skinny, ill-tempered, shitty weed of a thing. Bloody bites and kicks. Honestly, the bloody thing's more trouble than it's worth!"

None of that bothered me much because every horse I ever had anything to do with was a maniac.

"I might be interested in giving him a go."

The trainer's face showed pathetic gratitude. "Too right! He's got top prospects, this one. See Hayden, it's just I've got too much on my plate to bring him into line. He just needs a good firm hand, that's all! Someone like you."

"I couldn't agree more. How about fifty dollars a fortnight out of my dole cheque?"

"He's yours!"

And Appro let his inner feelings show, rearing and striking out with his front legs, trying to kill me or at the very least to maim.

At that time I was training under other people's names while I waited for my registration to come through and I didn't want to run Appro until then, because I knew he would win with the bomb and I wanted my name officially recorded as the trainer. But Bainsey was back in the picture with force and I should have known he wouldn't have a bar of it.

"Of course he's running! Now, come on, Hayden, the pub's down the bloody spout and we need the win!"

"You need the win."

"But I thought we were partners!"

"Look Bainsey, fair dinkum, I can't nominate as trainer and I haven't got anything to punt on him myself."

"A trainer's licence has never stopped you before! Look I'll give you whatever's left over when I pay out the pub debts, okay? Now, that's fair!"

I gave in, and Appro's first run for us was scheduled for a country meet over a fair distance, which suited the bomb down to the ground. The jockey's instructions were to hold him back as hard as he could, but the mongrel just wouldn't wear it. He was all over the track, right out wide, and my wife Monica (who knew nothing of the bomb) was shouting uncharacteristic obscenities at him until the jockey gave up the struggle and gave Appro his head. What a form reversal! After eight lasts he had bolted home at twenty-five to one and Bainsey was the only "idiot" on course who backed him.

I was still smarting because I would have liked the win under my name, and arguing with the bloke whose name I was using about who would lead Appro in. A steward settled the issue for us. He walked up behind and listened in on the conversation, then addressed the trainer formally.

"You, sir, lead the horse in," he said. Then he turned to me. "Haitana, into the Stewards Room."

Monica stared after me as I fell in behind.

"They can't take it away from us now, can they?"

"We'll be right, love," I replied softly, not understanding how they'd got onto my untraceable potion.

It turned out to be over something altogether different.

"We have an outstanding cheque here from your previous entry," he said, waving it under my nose, "and it's a dud."

"How much?"

"Thirty dollars," he said. "And don't think I'll be taking any of your cheques!"

I thought for a moment. If I had thirty dollars I'd have used it to back the horse.

"Well, you give me your cheque first, for the prize money, and I'll cash it to pay you."

The official sighed.

I always seemed to be up before the stewards for something, which was a worry because I still didn't have a trainer's licence, but on this occasion I reasoned it was worth it.

Bainsey had made a small fortune and I was in for the cream, but predictably, once he paid out all the pub's outstanding wages and bills and freshened up the stock, there was bugger all left. And it was a genuine pain in the backside, because my dole money was gone and I needed funds for a month's back payments on Appro.

We were in the pub and I was abusing Bainsey for conning me when suddenly he had a flash of brilliance. On a whim he turned and shouted across the bar.

"Anyone here want to rent a racehorse?"

He was met by dumb gazes then a chorus of "What?"

"A racehorse. It's simple. You pay up expenses and you get to be owner for the day at any meeting you choose. You take all the prize money, but your cash is up front because the horse is a proven winner."

Haitana's Rent-a-horse was officially open for business, and we were stunned by the response. Within a few minutes we had a list of names long enough to carry the bills for six months, and no problems apart from transport. Neither Bainsey nor I had a driver's licence at that stage, so there would have to be some other arrangement.

"I know!" said Bainsey. "We'll get cabs!"

"Oh, come on, mate! Some of those meetings are three hundred kilometres up the road. It'll look stupid. And what taxi driver is going to come at it?"

Bainsey laughed. He had tamed Port Adelaide's taxi drivers long ago. At times he had so many of them involved in various schemes that their public service suffered badly. After calling cab companies for half an hour without success, Monica sometimes phoned the pub demanding to know what we had done with them all.

We sent taxis all over the State to pick up horses and they'd often call up lost, or having rolled a float on some goat track supposed to be a road. Accidents in our company were common as Bainsey had a habit of changing his mind about destinations in midstream, but only two of them were at all serious, and typically, each was caused by drink. If the trip was long we'd make sure the back was well stocked with cans of beer, and if it was a marathon we loaded a keg in the boot.

A five hundred kilometre taxi ride to Moonee Valley was the first time we came unstuck, the cab crunching into the rear of another vehicle, though not hard enough to injure anyone. Our driver was so obviously plastered that his victims, who were uninsured, wanted to call the cops straight away. With immense cool Bainsey stepped into the fray.

"So you'll be paying for all that damage yourself then, eh?"

"Bullshit!" retorted the injured party, a nuggetty man in his thirties backed up by a fiercer looking wife. "This bloke should end up in jail!" He pointed to our driver being sick at the kerbside.

"You know the insurance won't pay if our driver is found to be under the influence, don't you? And he's only a casual. I can assure you he doesn't have a cracker you could sue him for. We'll fix up your damage on the cab's insurance all right, but I wouldn't go calling the cops!"

Bainsey was a tower of strength in such situations, but it was my daughter Mandy who next saved us. The cabbie on this occasion hadn't had all that much to drink, but he was over the limit when the cops pulled us up for speeding. They carted him off to the lockup, leaving us to take the cab home and work out some way to get him off.

"Mandy, you don't feel real well," said Bainsey suddenly.

I looked up, alarmed about my little girl, to see Bainsey grinning from ear to ear. A few minutes later we were off to see a tame doctor. We got the cabbie off the charge by producing a doctor's certificate which said Mandy may have died had that heroic taxi driver not offered to speed her to hospital!

The Rent-a-horse clients had been highly impressed by Appro's debut and were already counting their prize money when the first proud "owners" set off for the track. They watched their horse run a shocker. The scheme might have been terrific in principle but I sure wasn't wasting any supermix on it and Appro ran lousy races, one after the other.

"No, you guys just picked the wrong meeting!" I protested. "If only you'd waited another week, I'd have had him up good and proper!"

"Jeez, he'd have bolted home yesterday," Bainsey told the bar, "if only that bloody jockey had followed Hayden's instructions right!"

We were surprised just how far we could stretch the "if only's". For months the excuses flowed and were accepted, but then the grumbling started.

"If only, you reckon! If only you bastards never conned us into this in the first place!"

Business dried up until, at last, a syndicate of renters who had their names down on the list pulled out, just before Appro was entered to race in a carnival at Mount Gambier. I still didn't have enough material to make a proper bomb but we figured Appro was about ready to try again, so Bainsey and I financed the meet ourselves.

I had a gutless old Valiant with suspect brakes — in fact the back brakes didn't work at all — but by now we were six thousand in debt to one cabbie alone and none of them would consider towing us to Mount Gambier. I had to risk it myself and the first disaster struck only a little way outside Adelaide.

Travelling through a small town, a Volvo made a hard right turn in front of me and my tired old brakes weren't up to the challenge. There was no way I could stop, towing the horse, and after the crash I had to walk back an entire block to return the Volvo's bumper bar. And it was only the nightmare start of a nightmare journey.

Outside the very next town I was making slow progress uphill when a truck loaded with gravel came hurtling around the next bend, out of control. He missed the car but sideswiped the float, panicking Appro so badly he reared up, broke his halter, and hurled himself out the back. The truck kept driving, the horse bolted and I had to round up a posse of local farmers willing to risk life and limb to help me catch him. I was hoping against hope that he wasn't injured but when we finally caught sight of him he was limping. Appro had had a bad leg to start with, so I wasn't sure he would be able to race.

It was bloody miserable, pulling the trailer together with fencing wire, nothing but petrol money in my pocket, gambling on a bombless horse for prize money only, and not a cent to punt. The most sensible thing would have been to turn right around but I had three days up my sleeve and I knew that if Appro wanted to win, and was angry enough to win, he bloody well would.

I started the car and ground the gears and we resumed our wheezing uphill run. We hit Mount Gambier late that night, in freezing cold and pouring rain, with nowhere to stay. Appro was so miserable he stood motionless all night with his head down, and that, at least, was a godsend, ensuring that he didn't further damage the leg. Nevertheless, the next morning it was so swollen he could barely walk. I managed to find us lodgings in a trotting stable and treated the injury with all I could afford—Epsom Salts and cold water. Neither Appro nor I were in much of a mood to work and if I had had money for a beer I would have gone to the pub and forgotten about it. My bedroom was a stables storeroom with a cement floor, I was living off baked beans again, and I had just enough money for the race entry fee. There was nothing left to get me four hundred kilometres home if Appro didn't place. I started to have this fantasy about taking Appro down to the abattoirs and eating him, just to pay him back. I dismissed it because Monica would kill me.

As soon as he could move I bandaged him up and started walking him around the trotting track, day and night. I doubted that too much more could happen to us, but the difficulties simply compounded. For a start some trotting official decided to make a big deal about having a galloper on a trotting track. After a few minutes of argument I became very angry.

"I'm the one that's galloping. He's trotting!" I shouted back, the sweat pouring off me, and thank heaven he had a sense of humour.

"Just so long as it's you!" he grinned, and moved off laughing, but I could have murdered him.

Next, a garbage truck spooked Appro in his stall and he ran headfirst into a brick wall. That was a massive headache for both of us. Then, and worst of all, I couldn't find a jockey prepared to ride him.

"Come on, Hayden!" they pleaded. "He's not fit to race and his form says he doesn't have a hope anyway. Give it away and we'll shout you a beer."

But on race day, who knows how, everything came together. I examined the list of jockeys in the paper and found a top apprentice from out of town riding just one race, and he took the mount. The tension made me feel ill but the time slipped away and there was Appro at the barriers, and then racing!

And they left him for dead, powering ahead until Appro was running last by a dozen lengths. So there, I thought. That was that. It was a ridiculous gamble from the start and I was blowed if I was going to watch him humiliate me further. I turned in disgust to walk away from it.

"But wait! Here's Appro making good ground from the rear!" came the call, and an urgency in the voice forced me to swing back. Appro's stride had lengthened and he had begun to gain rapidly. There didn't seem enough ground left to tackle the leaders but my heart was pounding as the leaders began to lose pace.

"One hundred metres to go and Appro going wide now and charging for the post!"

He was fourth, then third, then second and I felt faint. It was unbearable. A sob came to my throat. My palms slapped up to my cheeks. My teeth clenched.

"And it's Appro!" The caller was in a frenzy. "Appro by a nose!"

Then trainers and punters and jockeys were leaping fences to congratulate me, I was surrounded by people shaking my hand and slapping my back. It was paradise.

"Didn't I tell you? Didn't I say he was a champion!" I was screaming and laughing and crying all in the one moment.

"Hayden Haitana to the Stewards Office," bellowed the public address. The call seemed to echo across the course for a long, long time.

I flushed. I had won the race fair and square but it was odds on that they were going to take it away from me, and I had no idea why. The crowd of well-wishers evaporated as I racked my brains for an explanation. Was Epsom Salts illegal? I stumbled to the Stewards Room where the bright congratulations of the outside office people, however sincere, sounded awfully hollow.

"We don't have any record of your trainer's registration, Mr Haitana," the Chief Official said quietly. "We know that it is you training the horse, not the bloke whose name you have down on the papers."

He paused and looked. I didn't trust myself to say anything.

"I think you'd better come and see us next week to speed up the proper application."

"Of course."

I rubbed my eyes, feeling terribly, terribly weary. And then looked up at him, puzzled.

"But what about today? Does that mean the win is going to stand?"

"Oh yes, I'd say so," he smiled.

"Whoopee!"

I cashed the trainer's cheque with a bookie for petrol money, loaded up with cold pies and colder beer, and after a mighty effort involving half a dozen conscripts, a dented door, and a nasty bite, we managed to get the hero of the day into his float. It was definitely the end of my association with that crazy horse. I just couldn't take it any more, and gave him away for free.

That should have sealed the fate of the ailing Haitana's Rent-a-horse, but we were unwilling to let a good thing die altogether. Once the pub heard about my win there was new enthusiasm for the concept, but no longer any horse to rent. Bainsey saw that as a minor difficulty.

"We'll just rent out other horses. Whole stables of 'em!" he enthused.

"Bainsey? Are you all there? My friend, we don't have whole stables of horses."

"So who's to know?"

His idea was simple enough, although it did depend on the bomb. We told the bar that we were leasing horses just like we had been — on a one-day basis. The deal was that we would sublet these horses to bar patrons and do all the raceday work, if they paid our costs and a percentage of the prize money. Of course, there was never any intention on our part to day-hire anything, but the up-front money provided by our customers made handsome punting stakes. The beauty of the scheme was that with the bomb we could almost guarantee an occasional winner at good odds, and that gave us enough "prize money" to keep the bar interested. We did, however, have to make it clear that our patrons were not to be at the track on the day, because of certain legal difficulties involved in the subletting process.

At first attempt, we knew we were on to a winner. We duly collected our fees from the patrons. They were a little disgruntled that the first horse was a rank outsider, but it blitzed the field. The pub was happy, we were rolling in money, and whoever happened to have owned the horse was happy too. It was what the Americans call a "mortal lock", a no-lose situation, and it was happy days until we ran out of bomb.

"Well, that's that for a while," I said to Bainsey as we watched our latest selection romp home. "It'll be months before I can get another charge together."

"There's got to be a way," he replied fiercely.

"Well, we could back favourites, but the odds will be too short for us even to win enough "prize money", let alone make a profit."

"Unless we can work the odds up somehow. Listen, Hayden, what do you do when someone gives you a hot tip? Something super-secret that no one else knows about?"

"Back the arse off it, of course."

He broke into a broad smile, clenched his fists, and shook them.

"And what happens when the arse is backed off a particular horse?"

"Come on, Bainsey. Don't play games. The bookies spook and the odds crash."

"Which lifts the odds on the rest of the field, right? Even the favourite! We're home and hosed, Haitch! You and I are in the gossip-mongering business!"

"But we can't hope to spark off a bloody nationwide plunge with a few rumours, can we?"

"No, but we can take on the country circuit. Gossip spreads faster than wildfire in those small towns and there's bugger all outside interest. The bookies will never know what hit them. We put out a rumour that one of the outsiders is going to romp home, but back the favourite ourselves. The S.P.'s can't accuse us of anything because we've backed the favourite, and that's only natural!"

The scheme worked like this. The night before a country meeting we sent a scout into the local pubs to start up idle conversations at the bars:

LOCAL: "Where you from?"
SCOUT: "Adelaide. Just dropped up to back a horse."
LOCAL: "Got a good chance, has it?"
SCOUT: "It'll piss it in!"
LOCAL: "True? What's its name?"
SCOUT: "Nah, sorry, mate. It'll be all over town and the odds'll crash."

Then later, pretending to be blind drunk, the scout would sidle up to the local and wink at him—"Our Bowie in the third."

Meantime, Bainsey would be on the telephone to the publicans claiming to be the owner of Our Bowie, asking for a favour.

"See, the horse will win easily," was his standard line, "but can I call you to confirm it? Because there's no radio coverage of this one, and I want to put all the winnings on a metropolitan race straight after."

Phase Three was conducted on course. More scouts had been given a few hundred dollars each to scatter among the bookies with as much drama as possible—"What'll you give me on Our Bowie? He's gotta be worth better odds than that!"

Locals who had been waiting nervously for some sign of action on the horse would then leap in for their bets before the odds crashed, sparking a big plunge. Meantime the odds on the favourite would climb, slowly at first but steadily, as the bookies tried to encourage action away from the plunge. The S.P. bookies would be paying close attention to the sudden interest, and altering their own odds accordingly. Just before betting closed we would hit them with everything. The comedy came afterward when the telephone rang for Bainsey—calls from disappointed publicans to say his horse had died in the bum. He found it almost impossible to hold back laughter while he cursed savagely with the losers. It's no wonder so many people were trying to strangle him!

With a scheme like that you would think we could have made a quick quid and got out, but somehow we still managed to punt away everything we won. The days of the great pub rorts ended, as they had to, when a few of the country favourites failed to come home and our customers lost interest again, and when at last we had exhausted all other forms of financial supply,—loans, stock, till, and wages. Bainsey's bosses, tired of silly excuses and outrageous promises, gave him the sack, and both of us moved on. These days, I believe, Bainsey is going to Gamblers Anonymous, but personally I think he's merely gathering information from former gamblers, still lying in wait for the big one.

It was the beginning of a new decade, the eighties, and while Bainsey and I had earned the status of experts in our own particular brand of con, the results should have been sufficient to convince me that there is no future in scamming. Furthermore, done properly there's as much work in a good con as there is in a normal living.

I trained a few more horses with reasonable results until my old cycling injury caught up with me. My back went bad and I was in hospital off and on, living on an invalid pension. Through all those years Monica had stuck faithfully by me, rearing our three children and never complaining. It suddenly occurred to me how much the con had cost us—how much time I had spent away from my family. At the time I had thought no one really minded, but when Monica and I celebrated our twelfth year of marriage she presented me with two cakes: one with twelve candles, one with two.

"Out of all our anniversaries," she teased, "I've been here for the twelve and you've only made it to two!"

And now it doesn't look much like I'll make the next one either, due to an altogether different style of con and the man who perfected it, the man they call the Phantom.

Chapter Thirteen
THE PHANTOM

The pale blue eyes snapped at me.

"Quick, mate, into the wagon!" urged the Phantom, and he hurried to the driver's window for a quick conference with the solicitor.

"Are we going to the pub?"

"What?"

"I'm getting thirsty!" I said with a smile, but there was a hard edge to my voice. I wanted a beer, and the rush and the Phantom's cold approach had made me impatient. Then John Gillespie grinned his grin and I melted.

"We might have one or two, eh? The others are meeting us there."

"Top stuff!" I exclaimed, feeling as though I had won something.

In a few moments we were casing the pub to check for detectives, because Bobby North and John Dixon were worried about being seen with us in public. The Phantom couldn't give a damn about it, but he had made a promise to our co-conspirators.

Soon we were all together again, hooting about all that had happened to date. It was nonsense talk, beer garden talk and good fun, but I was sure the Phantom's big crunch was waiting, his new scheme, and it wasn't long before it came.

"So how are we going to pay for our legal costs?" asked Gillespie, his eyebrows raised, and we all exchanged glances. "Because I'll tell you what," he continued, "I think we could get away with another ring-in, up in Cairns. Security is just as bad up there and there's a lot of bookies fielding, so we could hit them all while the odds are good."

There was silence, as the Phantom studied each of us in turn.

"You've gotta be joking, Johnny," I laughed.

"But everyone's onto us," said an incredulous Bobby North.

"Well, it sounds bloody ridiculous to me," said John Dixon gravely, "going all the way to Cairns. I mean, isn't there some way of getting the money locally?"

"Well, if you've got something better, that's good," Gillespie shrugged, "but I think Cairns is the best way to go."

More silence, all of us thinking about the possibilities and the hazards and the logistics. I tended to think that the Phantom favoured Cairns because he felt confident there. Cairns is where he got his big start in the con.

Not many people know much about Gillespie's background but he says he grew up tough, canecutting around Ingham just south of Cairns in North Queensland, and doing some pro fighting on the side. You wouldn't think he was a bluer, because he looks more like a stockman, with the good-natured humour and sincere, honest manner of the classic Australian bushie. His innocent looks were part of his strength, because, as I had discovered, he was actually as cunning and ruthless as a sewer rat, in a nice kind of way, if that makes any sense. In other words he was a world-class con, with experience going back twenty years or so to the time he rang himself in for a Cairns boxing match.

It's a good story. He was up against the champion of Ingham's big Spanish community, and that was dangerous in itself, because they're emotional buggers and they take it personally if one of their mates loses. The fight was more complicated because Gillespie outclassed his opponent easily and since the Spaniards' patriotism didn't stretch as far as doing dough, all their money was on John. Their problem was that they couldn't admit it openly, so they were barracking for their bloke while at the same time hoping like hell he'd get beaten to a pulp.

After a while they didn't know where they were and that made them mean, but everything was in John's favour. He was, in fact, getting paid to take a dive, and the sneaky Spaniards couldn't get upset about it because if they did their mates would murder them. They couldn't exactly stand up and say their great champion didn't win fair and square, so John just had to make it look good for a while, lie down, and walk out with his pay, and the loot he'd got a mate to lay on the opposition. The problem was that the Spaniard fought dirty. After the bell sounded the end of the third round the bastard landed a couple of stingers which infuriated Gillespie.

He returned an open-handed clip which sent his opponent sprawling, the Spaniards called foul and, forgetting who their money was on, they surged up into the ring. John took care of them all right, one after the other, but then the police sergeant ordered a five minute cooling off period. Later, Gillespie and his manager were talking and laughing about the scheme in the dressing room, and they didn't know at the time that one of those sneaky Spaniards had been listening outside the door.

When the match resumed, John reckons you could have heard a pin drop. All the barracking had died right off which made him really worried, and in between rounds he told his manager to get the hell up in the gallery and find out what was going on. It was the last he ever saw of him.

"Good old Gus," Gillespie says. "When one of the bookies told him what had happened he was straight out the door, and I was left to face a couple of thousand big, tough, brawling, canecutting bastards with knives, and they were spewing!"

The only thing John could do was make it look good so he had to cop a hell of a hiding until the police sergeant, who had figured there could be trouble, arrived with reinforcements. The moment the cops were in position Gillespie lay down, and war broke out. He was off the mat almost as soon as he hit it, charging between the columns of police for the door. He finished up drinking with the cops all night, because the sergeant had heard something and backed the Spaniard too. The S.P. bookies didn't mind paying out because they made a small fortune when the favourite went down. John got hold of his takings and skipped town in a hurry.

And I'll give the Phantom this. He had a fair shot at honest living. For three years he was in the army, building his savings for the dairy farm he eventually bought near Nambour, north of Brisbane. But he couldn't hack a predictable life. He says he finally got inspiration from a pair of white shoes which everyone said made him look like a used car salesman, and that's the direction he headed in. Like a lot of people, I thought used car salesmen were the pits, but when I got to know the Phantom and he talked about it, you could see another side — the very basics of the con. I copped lectures three or four times, and they went along these lines:

"Used cars are the best training ground for a con there is, because you're working with people's self-image and no matter how hard their brains tell them not to, they really want to believe you. You say to some prospect: 'Gee, that's a great shirt!' Straight away the poor bastard is congratulating himself for being so bloody 'with it', and his defences are down."

When John put it like that I could see the logic, but I sure couldn't see myself in white shoes and a loud tie, and this really frustrated him.

"All that image isn't there by accident, because if you go up to some bloke who's in jeans and a body shirt, and you're all dressed up in a classy three-piece suit, it only makes him nervous. He'd be saying to himself 'How come this idiot can afford to dress like that?' and you screw up all the work you've done making him feel better and smarter than you. You've got to dress neat and clean, but tacky."

"Yeah, but how's that going to sell a car?"

"Well, it doesn't by itself but it's all the same principle. You point out whatever car you reckon he can't possibly afford, and you look envious, and suddenly he's got to prove how much better than you he thinks he is. He won't want to go down-market because he won't want to admit that that's all he can afford. So offer some kind of finance package that might make it possible for him to buy and he'll probably jump at it. It'll be a bucket of rust by the time he pays it off, but he's not thinking about that. He's got a gut full of butterflies, and he's imagining how much this car is going to do for his image, and he's psychologically backed into a corner, so you keep the pressure on. You shunt him into the office and call the finance crowd while he's there watching you, giving him encouraging looks the whole time. When you put the phone down you look him in the eye and say: 'They won't be in it.' And the prospect fair jumps down your throat. 'What?' he says, and you put a sad look on your face and tell him you'd have to drop the price by a few hundred and that means bugger all commission. Then you wait for a while to watch the effect, and say: 'Okay, it's yours', and the deal is closed."

That was the mind that gave us the Fine Cotton ring-in. No matter how it looked, that scheme had bugger all to do with horses or racing. They were unimportant bits that fitted in somewhere on the side. The Fine Cotton ring-in was all to do with weakness, not in the racing system or the legal system or any other system, but in people. The Phantom knew instinctively whether someone's character had a glass jaw or a soft belly, and the more glass jaws and soft bellies he could play off against each other, the slicker the game.

That's why he was obsessed with ring-ins. Because he had the heavies and the stewards and the punters and the bookies and the cons and the cops, all to toy with. One slight change of the rules and the whole complicated mess went topsy-turvy, and it was always the Phantom pulling the strings. It was a slick game, and in the end he had the lot of us sitting up and begging.

Chapter Fourteen
FINE COTTON

John Gillespie spent a long time thinking about ring-ins while he was locked up in jail. He had been on the verge of pulling his first ten or eleven years before, but the cops caught up with him at the last moment on the shonky finance deal which, ironically, was what had got him mixed up in ring-ins in the first place.

In his used car dealings he had set up a network of loan shark contacts, and after some time he was offered a job as manager of a Brisbane finance operation. The company was in a shambles because one of the directors was ripping it off blind, and when John uncovered the scheme he forced the bloke to outline the ropes of the rort in full. The director then took a permanent overseas holiday, but the scheme was still running well and the Phantom picked up the pieces where the director left off. The company's fortunes continued to decline and the police were moving in when Gillespie chanced on what he thought was a sure way out.

One of John's regular customers was in the old habit of borrowing a few thousand dollars, then having the whole loan paid off in a lump within a few days. It smelled to high heaven of a top scam and John refused to approve any more money until this fellow agreed to spill whatever it was. The borrower was clearly desperate and he instructed Gillespie to have the money ready for the next day's races, where he would outline the scheme. It involved ring-ins and one was about to come off, but sadly for John it was too late to get his own punting stake together for that meeting's event.

Instead, he talked his contact into a partnership. John was to supply funds through the finance company and his partner was to look after the organisational side. They were wild about it. Imagine having other people's money to bet on a stacked deck! The Phantom insisted on knowing the exact method of going about a ring-in, and swore that once one or two came off he would never work again.

"It would have been the greatest con of all time," he once sighed, "but before we could get another one organised the Fraud Squad moved in on the finance company and I was in prison. Boy, I was dirty!"

During his long stay in jail the Phantom thought constantly about ring-ins. He told fellow inmates that he was determined to have one hopping within a few weeks of his release, and so began to establish the network of underhand racing contacts which would be necessary.

Even inside, Gillespie had his key people selected. He needed a lieutenant with a close eye for detail, a runner who would perform his duties fast and without questions, and a trainer prepared to put his career on the line. Cons put him onto other cons, character references were exchanged, and abilities were discussed. Well before his release, Gillespie had his eye firmly fixed on a lieutenant called Robert North, a runner called John Dixon, and a trainer called Hayden Haitana.

Countless times I have wondered why, after I had given up the con, I was stupid enough to become involved in that ring-in. But I was vulnerable at the time, away from my family up in northern New South Wales visiting my elder brother Sonny, who was in Coffs Harbour on a working holiday. Sonny is as straight as a die and he would have stopped me or at least threatened to turn me in had he known of the deal. But the ring-in sort of crept up on me, and when at last I realised I was central to the plan I figured that since Sonny was a trainer himself, it was better he didn't know.

For a few months, life was rosy. I was back in the training business full time and Sonny had brought over a decent gelding called Roimac to clean up the locals. Our happiness was complete when Pat joined us, fresh out of Boggo Road Jail where he had landed after a typical display of temper. He had been thrown out of a Gold Coast football club, and had driven his car through the front windows in revenge.

The magistrate had sentenced him to six weeks inside. He managed to get one of the prison system's top jobs, in the officers' mess, which was unusual for a short termer, and when Pat told me about it I asked who he'd known with the influence to get him out of the laundry and into the kitchen.

"No one," he said. "I got quite a surprise myself, but the whole officers' mess was crammed with racing people. It turned out that the prisoner who ran the kitchen was trying to organise some kind of racing syndicate, and anyone coming in who had anything to do with horses got shunted straight up to him. Not that I was complaining. He reckons he needs a jockey and a trainer, and he's promised to come see us when he gets out."

"Is that so? Anyone I'd know?"

"I don't think so. His name's John Gillespie but they call him the Phantom. Ring any bells?"

"Nah. Forget about it anyway. People make all sorts of promises inside and they hardly ever come off, so I doubt you'll see him again. The Phantom you say? Sounds like a failed punter."

"White collar crim, actually. But I don't know. He sounded pretty keen and he reckoned he'd always go for an ex-con over someone straight."

We dropped the subject then, and thought no more about it.

Pat and I took a lease on a great, rambling, roomy property just outside Coffs Harbour. We had rented stables at the track, both of us were doing pretty well and we were fairly well regarded, despite our records. Pat was riding winners, I had three good prospects in my stables, and we began to give serious thought to bringing our families up and settling there for good. There was an honest living to be made and best of all we would be away from the kind of people that always steered us into trouble. It would be a fresh start and the kind of settled life we had been looking for. Then one night, when we were drinking peacefully at a Coffs Harbour hotel, along came smooth-talking John.

Pat was drinking with his jockey friends at a table and I was over at the bar when Gillespie walked in. I noticed him because he was a stranger in a locals' pub, but I thought nothing of it until Pat came over to buy a round of drinks.

"Remember that Phantom bloke I met in jail? John Gillespie? The one I said was interested in hiring us? That's him in the corner. He wants a word with you."

I looked over to the stranger, who was staring at us with a set of very pale blue eyes. He raised his hand from the table and smiled.

"What's he like? Is he a good payer?"

'Yes. He seems to have plenty of money and he's a top bloke too. He's a good mate of one of the other local trainers."

"Why doesn't he take his business there, then?"

"Well, I don't rightly know. Remember I said that he likes ex-cons?"

"Yes. All right. I suppose we can handle two more."

I wandered over to this Phantom and our conversation was as simple as saying I'd take the job, but that he could deal through Pat. He was likeable enough, but he only had one horse and I was with friends not interested in wasting good drinking time on a stranger.

I heard nothing more about it for a week or so, and had dismissed John Gillespie as just another big noter, until on a freezing night at about two in the morning, a float was towed up to the house and I woke at the sound of a horn. It was a hell of a night, black as pitch and pouring rain, and I stumbled outside to see this poor animal with no rug, shivering in an open float. It was eerie. I had the feeling that nothing about this business would make any sense and I shuddered inwardly with something like a premonition. There were two figures in the front seat, masked by a foggy windscreen, neither of them moving. They just sat there in the driveway as though they were expected. I dragged on a set of oilskins and gumboots and sloshed to the passenger window.

"This the Haitana place?" a young fellow shouted over the rain, and I nodded.

"What do you want?"

"We got a horse for you from John Gillespie. Fine Cotton. He's a bit of a bastard to handle but we'd be bloody grateful if you could get him out by yourself."

"Well, if he was toey before, he won't be now. He'll be stiff as a board. Where'd you come from?"

"Wellington. Bloody back of beyond."

The fools had towed him all day and half the night, and I was flabbergasted.

"Why the open float? Why no rug?"

"Well, he didn't have a rug and we didn't want to stop because he's just too bloody difficult to handle. Like we said, you might have trouble getting him off."

"Too bloody right!" I shouted, really angry now. "He'll be frozen.

When they get like that they can't move. They can't even bloody piss!"

"Listen, don't blame us, okay? It's just our instructions from John."

I stalked around to the back of the float and in the darkness I caught my first glimpse of the sorriest creature I have ever laid eyes on. Fine Cotton, drenched, and shaking, without a trace of spirit left in him. I walked him carefully from the float, talking to him gently, trying to keep him moving, and he followed me like a lamb. I showed him where the water was, and guided him right along the perimeter of the barbed wire fence so he wouldn't plough into it if he was spooked. I tried to lead him into what served as a stable, a corrugated iron shelter, but the rain pelting on it made such a racket he wouldn't go near it. It was hours of drenching bitter cold before I felt confident he would survive the night. I left his feed out under a tree in the paddock and went back to bed fuming about the callous ignorance of anyone who could put any creature at all through that kind of treatment.

The day dawned bright and track work started at five, so I didn't take another look at Fine Cotton until midmorning. He was a big, dark bay, sixteen and a half hands high, and he looked much better in the daylight. He was calm as a kitten and my track rider hopped straight up and gave him a good workout through nearby forest, reporting that he would make a great jumper to go back to Adelaide with and still had good potential as a galloper. At this stage I had no idea how the owner intended to campaign him, so I started him on a course of vitamin and hormone injections and mapped out a training schedule.

As the days passed I grew strongly attached to Cotton and, with all due modesty, I think he was impressed by me too. I was pleased with his progress and looking forward to giving his owner a highly favourable report, so I was shattered when, a week later, the Phantom dropped his bombshell. Without any notice he called by in the morning, and eyed the horse appreciatively.

"How's he going, Hayden?" he asked, like butter wouldn't melt in his maw.

"Great! He's a winner, this bloke, for sure. You've got to wake him up at the track but when he gets going he's a flyer!"

Gillespie pondered. "Problem is, we don't want him to win," he said, and he fixed me with a sincere gaze. "He's going to be part of a ring-in."

I had great difficulty swallowing a mouthful of beer already on its way down. It was suddenly obvious why Gillespie wanted to deal with ex-cons and why he didn't give a damn about Cotton.

A ring-in is a complicated con to set up, but simple in principle. Horses are raced in a variety of classes to keep the competition even, because in theory every horse should have a chance of winning. For example novices run against other novices and the well-performed, open class horses run against other open class horses. As an animal's performance improves, it graduates from one class to the next. The guts of a ring-in is that an open class horse entered in a novice race is a certainty to win, but as that's obviously against the rule, the rules have to be broken: a ring-in is when a novice is entered in its correct class, but a better performed, look-a-like horse is substituted to run the race instead. As you can be pretty sure the substitute will win, there's no risk in betting everything you have on it.

"Christ!" I said, when I recovered from a fit of coughing. "What's going on here?"

And Gillespie outlined his plan. He told me that he had spent weeks looking for the right horse, one nearing the end of its racing career so it wasn't too expensive; an ordinary-looking horse that no one had heard of and no one would look twice at. It had to come from somewhere in the country so that no city person would be familiar with it. Otherwise there was the chance that some punter or racecourse steward would realise, on the day, that another horse had been substituted for it. There was also the advantage of an unknown having no metropolitan track record so, if you could race it very poorly a few times before the ring-in, the odds would climb. It also had to be eligible to run in a novice event (meaning it had won less than a certain amount of prize money), and have no special distinguishing marks that would make it hard to find a look-a-like.

"I had to scour the whole of western New South Wales for it," complained the Phantom, "and you wouldn't believe how I found him. I was at Wellington, out near Dubbo, looking through the racebook, and I saw this one called Fine Cotton. But there were miles of stalls so I had no idea where to find him. When I asked one of the strappers if he knew where this Fine Cotton was, he turned around to the stall right behind us and said: 'That's him there.' The damn thing was staring at me! I was a bit dumbfounded, but he looked the part, and I asked the strapper to get me his trainer. I figured he'd be worth about twelve hundred but when it turned out he wasn't really for sale because he was a bit of family pet, I offered them two grand and they leapt at it."

I had already decided to steer well clear of this one. My training career was just off the ground again and I didn't feel like risking a scam with someone I didn't know. But for a moment, my con man's curiosity got the better of me. I walked around to face Cotton and stroked his nose.

"You putting the money up then, are you?" I said to Gillespie. A ring-in needs fair backing to buy both horses, stable and feed them, to train the substitute, to buy help, and to pay off whoever needs to be paid off.

"No," said Gillespie. "Don't you worry about that. That's not your worry." That was fine by me because you don't want to go poking your nose around those sorts of things. I'd learned that from the dockers. What I wanted to know next was, why me? The Phantom paused for a moment and smiled.

"Actually there's another bloke tied up in this—John Dixon—that we tried first. We sent him off to register with the racing club and the poor bastard came back shaking. They asked him all sorts of questions like 'Where'd you serve your six months as a strapper?' and 'Who are you training for?' John knows nothing at all about racing. He says he back-pedalled so fast he almost went over the receptionist's desk! He reckons we're not supposed to do that sort of stuff to him anymore, but at the time, well, it was worth a shot."

"But if I get your drift, you don't want me to train Fine Cotton at all. You want him to run lousy."

"That's right. But we've got to give him a few starts first to get him properly known in Queensland, and get through the red tape and stuff. We'll need a trainer to front for that. But you're right, the worse he runs in the lead up, the better the odds will be on the day."

I was interested suddenly, because I could see a way of being involved in the scam without taking any of the actual risk myself.

"When's the ring-in supposed to be?" I asked. "And what have you done about getting the other horse?"

"Listen, I'll tell you what, Hayden. You leave the details to me and I'll let you know in plenty of time. You want to be in it?"

"Well, not like you're saying, because I've just renewed my licence and I look like having a couple of good winners shortly. But I tell you what I will do. I'll front as the trainer until just before it comes off, if you'll get someone else to saddle him up on the day."

Gillespie sniffed and folded his arms. He turned away and walked a full circuit of Fine Cotton, deep in thought, then unfolded his arms and offered me his hand.

"Put it there, Hayden. Partner."

"My friends call me Haitch."

"Righto, Haitch. I'll let you know when his first race is. Give you plenty of notice. And as soon as I get hold of the substitution I'll get him down here. That one, we want trained up good and proper!"

For the moment I was pleased with the bargain. It was a fair sort of deal, getting in on the edge of a good money spinner without taking the risk. I hoisted myself up onto Cotton and invited my new partner into the house for a beer, laughing to myself about how much Bainsey would love a piece of it. But the truth was I shouldn't have been thinking about Bainsey. I should have been remembering a valuable lesson taught to me by another of my partners in scam, a cagey 'hitinerant' called Eddie!

Chapter Fifteen
BUNDAMBA

When the Phantom left late in the afternoon both of us were well under the weather. I strolled out into the paddock for another look at Cotton. His muscles were already swelling hard with the training, his head was up, yet still there was that endearing gentleness about his eyes. I knew very well that I couldn't let him go downhill. My trainer's instincts were greater than the Phantom would ever understand, and I was certain that with a good bit of work I could get him fit enough to win the race on his own merits, without the ring-in. I liked the horse and besides, I wasn't too fussed with the notion of any of my charges running last by twenty lengths. I had my own reputation to uphold and was on the verge of success with my other horses.

The Phantom didn't exactly live up to his end of the bargain either. His "plenty of notice" of Fine Cotton's first entry, at Bundamba racecourse near Brisbane, was less than twenty-four hours. The float arrived out of the blue late one afternoon, a beaten up hulk of a thing with bald tyres. The drivers who delivered it cleared out before I had much of a chance to talk to them, but I gathered it was essential that Cotton run on the following day, bugger it! We had to get going quick smart, so that both of us got a decent night's sleep at the course, and Cotton had a chance to feed. He was a night feeder, Fine Cotton. He wouldn't touch his hay during the day but at night you could pick out his silhouette, hoeing into the mix. Not much more than half an hour later we were heading north, trying to make Bundamba in the light.

What I reckon should have been a five or six hour trip turned into a twenty-hour marathon. The old, beaten up Holden John had sent me could barely pull the float. Just north of Grafton, one of the trailer's back wheels flew off. I might have known that the spare wouldn't fit, and I wasn't able to lead the horse out without the risk of tipping the float. It meant that I had to hitch to and from Grafton, and then there was the difficult job of repairing the float with the horse actually in it. Fine Cotton took the process placidly and again I felt my heart go out to him. An Appro or Real Chamozzle would have kicked the float to matchwood. Repairs and the rest of the journey took most of the night, and by the time we made the track the poor horse was starving. There was no time for feed and barely enough time to get his shoes on, and that was how he would race, tired and hungry.

John Gillespie beamed, all done up in a coat and tie, looking fresh and relaxed.

"Jeez, you've done a good job, Hayden," he said. "He looks knackered!" I glared back at him and he changed the subject.

"Now, here's what you've got to do. We'll need him checked over by the stewards, right? Don't we need to get his papers looked at?"

I nodded, my eyes red with fatigue and my hands blackened with axle grease.

"That's good, because when we have to forge his papers later to fit the other horse's description, we can copy the signature."

I mumbled agreement and bumbled off to find a steward. Despite my attempts to attract attention, it was only at the last moment I managed to find an official to check the papers.

My heart was in my mouth because I really wanted Cotton to win but I couldn't see it happening because he was so buggered. Everything worked against him. He drew wide, which can be quite a disadvantage, he had a heavy weight, and John had made sure I instructed the jockey not to pull the whip on him. And still he ran a race to be proud of. That gutsy, beautiful animal led around the home turn, but halfway up the straight he tired and fell back through the field. The Phantom turned to me, smugly self-satisfied.

"Good one, Haitch! I bet we see better odds on him next time."

"The next start you'll see him bloody win," I replied.

Under the circumstances Cotton's performance had been brilliant, and I knew that wouldn't have escaped Gillespie's attention. It was then I decided to take a chance on showing my hand.

"Honestly, John, this bloke could be a champion out in the bush. Why pull a ring-in when you could back him fair and square."

"I don't like fair and square," he said. "I like to be sure. You can race Cotton yourself in Ballina if you like, but after the ring-in!"

"How long?" I gulped, a catch in my voice. That horse was all the payment I could have asked for!

"We'll give him a few starts in the next couple of weeks, pull the job, and then he's yours. Okay?"

But the Phantom had firmly caught on how I felt about the horse and that meant immediate changes in his strategy. By the time we had loaded Cotton into his float John was sure that no matter what instructions he gave me, I would go ahead and train the horse my way. He was beautifully casual about it, smiling his mischievous smile, running his hand through his hair.

"I'll tell you what, Haitch old mate. Pat warned me you were a hell of a good trainer and I'm starting to believe him."

I laughed along with him, a sucker for flattery, and as the laughter and the sighs died away he raised his eyebrows and slapped me on the shoulder.

"It's a bloody shame about last night, eh? It must have taken a bit out of the horse. And he's going to have a fair schedule ahead of him, you know. Maybe we'd be better off giving him some quarters closer to town, say the Gold Coast. That would save you floating him so far, wouldn't it?"

I had to agree that it made sense.

"Well now, I don't want to put you at any disadvantage with your other horses either, Hayden, seeing as they're good prospects and all, and you can't be shuffling back and forth to the Gold Coast every day. So I've just had a word to a mate of mine who's got a place at the Coast, and he's taking Cotton over. We'll just get you up on racedays, eh?"

I fumed all the way to Coffs Harbour but there had been nothing to argue about. We wanted Fine Cotton to run lousy and I had other work to get on with. It was just so—disappointing!

I was concerned. Days had passed with no contact from the Phantom and I began to realise how little I knew about the con I was involved in. I had developed a strong suspicion that Gillespie would have agreed to just about anything I might have said to have me in on the ring-in, but living up to his promises could easily be a different matter. I began to have serious doubts that there was ever any intention to let me bail out. Where was he going to find another trainer willing to put his name to an unknown horse, on behalf of unknown people, at the very last moment? It would reek of a rort. And even if some other trainer did go along with it, if the ring-in went wrong on the day and the shit hit the fan, it would be mighty difficult not to get splattered.

Gradually a smart plan of action took shape in my mind. If there was a double cross—and it was a very strong chance—there was still one way out. If Gillespie did put the weights on me to saddle the horse on the day, I was already in the con so far that I would almost certainly have to go along. But that would allow me an alternative which the Phantom hadn't considered, and which he couldn't do a thing about. That old sixth sense screamed "Run!", but there was plenty of time. Plenty of time, and a last resort. And I still had the chance to get my itching hands on that horse called Fine Cotton.

Chapter Sixteen
Mortal Lock

The following weekend John Gillespie and Bobby North arrived at my place in Bob's gold Mercedes sports, pulling a float that carried a horse called Dashing Soltaire. It was the ring-in, an open company horse of fairly plain appearance with a good record.

But once that was established I didn't know which to be more interested in, the horse or Bobby North. It was the first time we had met and I was fascinated by the contrast he made with John. The Phantom was, as always, calm and unruffled, while Bobby was highly animated, a super-fast talker in high class clothes and thick gold jewellery. They were an odd couple all right!

Apparently Dasher had been on ice for some time, but as the ring-in was imminent they had towed him over from a nearby property to go undercover while I trained him up to make sure he won.

"And he's a stayer, John?" I asked, giving the horse a good look-over.

"No, he's a sprinter."

I left the horse to walk over to the Phantom, and study his face carefully. In the lead up to the ring-in we had planned to enter Fine Cotton in distance events only, so I had assumed that the ring-in race would be the same.

"We're going to substitute a sprinter for a stayer in a distance event?"

"That's right, so you'll have to retrain him for it."

But horses don't retrain easily, especially in just a few weeks, and under those circumstances there was no way that I could guarantee a win. As far as I could see, commonsense had left us in favour of fantasy. I shook my head gravely.

"It's bloody madness. If that's what's going to happen, I wouldn't have a cent on him myself."

"Here's the horse, mate," said Gillespie with finality. "They say you can work miracles, and I'm bloody sure of it. Pat reckons you could bring a horse back from the dead, and he'll give you a hand with it, won't he?"

That added fat to the fire. I had tried to talk to Pat about the Fine Cotton thing a few nights before, but as soon as I mentioned Gillespie's name he had turned his back and said that whatever was going on he didn't want to know.

"That's another thing, John. Pat's out of this. He won't be riding for you."

The Phantom grinned his maddening grin.

"Pat was never in it, Haitch. I've already got a jockey in mind and he doesn't know what's going on either! Look we've already given Dasher a run in an open sprint at Grafton. He came a good fourth. He'll be all right."

"Well, let's say it isn't all right and he gets beaten. I hope you won't be holding me responsible, because right now I'd be out looking for another horse! I reckon his front feet are sore at the moment, and if you ask me Cotton's got a better chance of winning than he does. If I could only get my bloody hands on him."

Gillespie was unruffled and Bobby North, who had been listening intently, entered the argument.

"Listen Hayden, there's already been ten grand forked out for him, and there's no money left to buy another one. John thinks he's a sure thing. The only thing you have to do is make sure he's fit and all right for the race. That's all you have to do."

That was all I had to do. The argument could have continued indefinitely but I was thirsty for a drink and grateful there was no mention of me fronting as trainer on the day. I could only do my best with Dasher, and it was their lookout from then on. I silently resolved that the training of my own horses wasn't going to suffer at the expense of Dasher, either.

"Righto, chaps. How about a beer?"

"Not for me, thanks, Hayden," said Bobby. "Have you got something soft?"

I stared at him like he was from another planet and the Phantom chuckled.

"Would you put drink into a body like that?" he grinned, waving at Bobby's admirable physique. "Listen, we've got some business to look after, Haitch. Cotton's next start is at Bundamba again, on Monday. Now, make sure you tell him to lose!"

Despite his lack of training, I was still enthusiastic about Fine Cotton's chances of doing well and obviously the Phantom thought so too, because the instructions he telephoned to me on Monday morning were outrageous.

"Now listen, Hayden. If we're going to get the odds up this horse has got to bomb badly today . . ."

I smiled to myself because if I put a bomb up him the horse would streak home!

". . . so I want you to give him a good hit out over a couple of miles before you come up to Bundamba."

"Right!" I said but thinking "No way".

"And I'll have a mate of mine there to make sure you do. I'm sorry, but I want him tired, knackered, finished, history. So gallop him flat out."

When it was arranged like that I didn't have a great deal of choice, so Fine Cotton got his hit out and he looked jaded as hell when we loaded him for the drive to Bundamba. And then something occurred to me. Something that made me grin, then smile, then giggle, then roar with laughter. Fine Cotton was a country horse. A long way up country a horse is often called on to run two races in the same day. That meant that despite the morning's hit out, Cotton shouldn't be the least bit bluffed by a second run. In fact, he would be in his element!

When I met John at the track he had already received the message that the job was done and he was happy as a lark. It was good to be able to laugh with him and sound genuine about it, because he can smell a rat a mile away. Hell, I felt clever, looking forward to a proper indication of how Cotton would run, and John was obviously pleased to see me in high spirits.

"That's more like it, Haitch!" he said. "Bloody good to see a smile on your dial!"

Gillespie would have screamed if he'd known I was conning him, so I carefully changed tack when we had a look at the horse.

"He's bloody tired, John," I moaned while the Phantom smiled his smug smile. "He's got no bloody chance at all!"

Gillespie's face was priceless as Fine Cotton shot out of the barriers, straight up with the leaders, and the commentator roared with enthusiasm. "Out wide, Fine Cotton showing speed to go up with the leaders! In fact, he's showing blistering speed!"

Gillespie turned to look at me, his face a mask of horror.

"He can't win. We can't afford a win," he whispered fiercely.

"That's a problem, all right. You just can't keep a good horse down."

But again, Cotton lost pace on the home stretch and fell back to finish middle field, but I knew that with a bit of proper training I'd soon improve his wind. The Phantom was happy enough with the final result but was even more determined to keep me away from Fine Cotton.

"Haitch," he said, tugging on an earlobe, "you've just lost a horse."

I feigned confusion.

"I thought I already lost it."

"No, I mean really lost it! I want you to stay away from it altogether. I'll have someone else pick him up and just meet you at the track from now on."

"Fair enough," I smiled. I was so delighted with his performance nothing could bother me, and then my best poker face was grinning from ear to ear. "But don't forget I want him after the ring-in. We'll win heaps with this one on the country circuit."

I stayed at the Gold Coast with Gillespie that night and he was like a kid, bubbling with mischief and greed as we drank steadily, discussing track security. I had to agree that it wasn't all that tight in Queensland, but the system of pre-race checks still had me worried — for the sake of whoever was fronting as trainer on the day, that is.

"Well, I meant to talk to you about that, Hayden," said the Phantom, his eyes wide with innocence, and he began to fill me in on the fine details of the scam. Casually, glowing with drink, he spoke about stewards and cops and forgers, but I knew damn well what was coming. The Phantom doesn't give out information unless it's absolutely essential.

"I've got some of the stewards on side," he said, "and they'll all be betting on Fine Cotton too, so there's no worries at the track. They'll all make sure they're looking the other way."

"Top stuff. You can't go wrong then."

"That's right. And the same goes for the cops because I've set up to pay them off. They'll be backing the horse too."

"Brilliant," I said, though by now I was starting to wonder just how much of this was the truth.

"And I've got some super-straight people signed up as owners, too."

"Are they in on it as well?"

"Don't know a thing. That's the beauty of it. No one would suspect these people of pulling a stunt, least of all themselves, so they can't give it away by getting nervous or anything."

That one confused me. I could see the soundness of signing Cotton over to respectable people, but surely they'd look at the horse beforehand as owners like to, and see that it wasn't theirs. Gillespie picked up on it straight away.

"No, Hayden, I know what you're thinking, but the registered owners have never even seen the bloody horse. Their shares were presents from friends!"

"Incredible!"

I had to admire the Phantom—but abruptly that admiration turned to horror. I started to sweat. I could feel his eyes on me and that made it worse!

"But will you be able to get Cotton back off them? For me to race?"

The Phantom sat forward, and took a swig of his stubby.

"Well, given time I'm sure I can, but see, Hayden, the problem might be when they think it's Cotton that has won the race. They'll want to put him with whoever was fronting as the trainer on the day. At least for a while."

"But who is fronting as trainer?" I asked, my anxiety getting the better of me.

Snap! He had me. I couldn't bear the thought of someone else with his mits on my horse. I sat there for a while with eyes cast down and the Phantom waited serenely for me to sweat it out—to state the obvious. Next thing, I would be begging for reassurance.

"And you reckon this whole thing is a mortal lock, eh?"

He knocked the top off another beer and handed it to me. "What's a mortal lock?"

Oh, for God's sake! He was playing it cool now, letting me dangle and thoroughly enjoying it. I tried to be calm.

"That's when even if everything that can go wrong does, you still can't lose."

"Yeah, that's a fair enough way to put it," he said brightly. "Nothing much can happen with the whole course on side."

"Yeah, all right. I'm your trainer."

"Hey! That's great! Let's have another on it."

So I had been quite right and the Phantom had always intended me to go the whole way. All that bothered me was that I had expected to hold the aces. And it was a worry to realise how easily I had been manoeuvred. The moment Gillespie realised he had a problem with my affection for the horse he had worked out a way to use it, to twist it to his advantage. It was so bloody typical of the man! But if nothing could go wrong, where was the harm? And I still held an ace, undisclosed.

The following day, I was with Gillespie on the Coast when our ring-in, Dashing Soltaire, ran straight through a barbed wire fence, badly injuring one of his hind legs. A strapper called the vet out and he reported that poor old Dasher would be out of action for months. I took the telephone call and it lifted a huge weight from my shoulders. Dasher couldn't race no matter what the Phantom said, and that meant breathing space. We either went with Fine Cotton or canned the whole thing.

"You're sure, Hayden?" Gillespie was uncharacteristically nervous.

"Yeah. Sorry, John, but there's no way he'll race. You'll have to call it off. Either that or I've got some dope that doesn't show up in a swab. The 'patent Haitana bomb'. We could pump it into Cotton and he'd win hands down."

DAMN it! There went the ace!

"What?" asked the Phantom quietly, his mind in overdrive. "What have you got?"

"It's this stuff they developed over in Kiwi. Gives a horse heaps more stamina and doesn't show up."

"Listen. Don't you tell anyone about this. Not a soul, right?"

"As far as I'm concerned the whole thing's forgotten."

"It's still got to be a ring-in, but whatever horse we end up with—you hit it with that stuff to make sure."

"Why not just put it in Cotton?"

"Don't you worry about it," he said. "You leave it to me and it'll be all right."

As I drove back to Coffs Harbour I figured I hadn't done too badly. I had lost my ace and I had got into the scam much, much deeper, but at least I had a month or so to think while they drummed up another ring-in. By that time I could be back in Adelaide if it got too heavy, but bloody hell, I sure did want that horse!

That same day, back in Coffs, the trainer who had Fine Cotton was on the telephone.

"You know Fine Cotton is entered at Doomben tomorrow, don't you?"

I had a moment of sheer panic because you simply don't race a horse—even a picnic horse—two days out of three. But I calmed down, remembering that Dasher was out of action and the plans would have changed.

"No, that wouldn't be right. That's a mistake. Give John Gillespie a call."

"I was just speaking to him."

I was jolted by the realisation. Racing a horse twice in a couple of days draws attention—the kind of attention that every con worth his salt tries desperately to avoid. If the Phantom was prepared to risk attention it meant there was no change of plan, no breathing space, and the ring-in was still imminent! But as far as I knew there was no substitute horse. As far as I knew the great Fine Cotton ring-in was gelded!

"You there?" said the trainer.

"Yes," I snapped. "It's stupid. Cotton only raced yesterday!"

"I told John it's awfully tough on the horse, and no one at the track is going to think much of it, but he wouldn't discuss it. He said it's going to race and that's that. I was supposed to call and let you know."

"That's because he wouldn't bloody dare say it himself!"

It was a hell of a jam. It would take time for John to buy another horse which could serve as a feasible ring-in—which was close to the same age, unknown, a certainty to win a novice, and a Fine Cotton look-a-like, but if the schedule was so tight it warranted attention-grabbing stupidity to cram in another run, the con had to be scheduled for the following Saturday. No question about it.

If that wasn't bad enough, my reputation would be lower than mud on course, because you can kill a horse that's a tryer by racing it too hard. Even jockeys and strappers and trainers who've had nothing to do with an animal take any kind of mistreatment personally, and they're not shy about letting you know. As I hadn't a clue what the Phantom could be up to, I had no choice but to roll with the punches, but he was going to hear about it. Boy oh boy, was he going to hear about it!

When we met at Doomben, Gillespie was patient but determined.

"Look," he sighed, "the ring-in was supposed to come off on Saturday and now it bloody can't and I'm in a lot of trouble that there's no need for you to know about. Now, I've still got Cotton entered for Saturday, but . . ."

"You're joking!" I exclaimed, then lowered my voice as the Phantom winced. "It'll be all over the course that we're driving him into the ground."

Gillespie continued impatiently, as though he hadn't heard me. "We'll scratch him this Saturday and go for the weekend after, but for the moment it's still got to look like it's all happening to plan, because I haven't worked out how to tell everyone else about the problem yet."

"Well, why not forget about today and go ahead as planned. We can race Cotton on Saturday with the bomb in him. He'll win, and it's over. Finished!"

"Listen, Haitch," said Gillespie with venom, "get off my back about canning the ring-in, will you? I've got enough to worry about, with every course in the country organised for a plunge on Fine-bloody-Cotton in three days' time!"

"That's rough!" I said bitterly. "You should have your horses ready before you organise the punt. Not vice-versa!"

We argued for half an hour or so and considering his position I had to admire John's cool. He gave many reasons why we had to race Cotton that day. "The stewards who check him over will be the same ones at Eagle Farm, so they won't pay close attention to him there." "Another bad performance will bring the odds up better for the plunge." And so on. When we ran out of time Fine Cotton went ahead and raced, a mediocre run, and afterward the Phantom was much more cheerful.

"You just leave it to me, Haitch!" he said over the froth of a beer. "There's a week and a half yet, and I'll get you another horse."

That Wednesday was the last time Fine Cotton ever raced on a registered course, but he still had to be entered for the following Saturday and word quickly spread among the ranks. Four races in less than two weeks! It looked like cruelty, and I had to cop a hiding over it.

"Horse killer!" a strapper shouted as I loaded Fine Cotton onto the float.

"No, he's all right," I stammered. "He's fit as a fiddle, this one!"

"Bullshit!" bellowed a jockey who had appeared from nowhere. "If he's so fit he wouldn't have run so poor today. Not with his potential."

It was just bloody awful. I couldn't bring myself to put up any further defence because they were right.

There were a few things about this scam that I was starting not to like. It had an unpleasant flavour to it. Even if all officialdom was in on the act (and that was getting a bit hard to believe anyway), the professional punter is a cagey bird and he knows his horses. The new ring-in had to be just right, and the Phantom now had less than two weeks to find it. That's what was so queer. While John might have been a master of the con, when something as drastic as losing your ring-in happens even the best get jittery; yet there wasn't a hint of doubt, or trace of concern, or inkling of annoyance or even the slightest sign of nerves.

But there was this. I was in up to my neck, and there was one thing about the ring-in that I did like and that was Fine Cotton himself.

Chapter Seventeen
BOLD PERSONALITY

Thursday and Friday came and went, then Saturday, Sunday, Monday, Tuesday and Wednesday, and that made a whole week with no contact from the Phantom. I guessed he simply wasn't able to find another horse and I was well back into the stride of my normal training commitments. I was so sure that the ring-in had been shelved that I even considered entering my own charges somewhere on Saturday. But the following morning it came, a telephoned cryptic message on behalf of the Phantom.

"Mr Haitana?" the caller said, over long distance pips.

"Hayden here."

"Message from John. Fine Cotton entered at Eagle Farm, Saturday, race four. It's on."

"Yes, hold up a sec . . .!" I began, but the caller had rung off. I put the receiver back and sat for a moment on a vinyl pouffe, staring at the wall. It was then just more than forty-eight hours before a sting which Gillespie had hinted was a biggie, and the person he was depending on to bring it together, and to take the rap if it failed — me — didn't have a clue what was going on.

"Good one, Johnny!" I said to the wall. "Top flight, my bum!"

It was one of those times they talk about when you don't know whether to laugh or cry, but after a short while, laughter won. I laughed until the tears came, not knowing . . . not knowing anything! I wasn't even sure we had our hands on another ring-in yet, and I could just imagine some confused kid showing up late as hell on Saturday morning, towing a derelict float behind a motorbike, wanting to pick up "Dashing Soltaire for Eagle Farm — Urgent!" quoting "Mr Gillespie's instructions!"

But if the Phantom wasn't prepared to worry about it, neither was I. We Haitanas are just not the worrying kind, and for better or worse I figured to cruise through whatever came like it wasn't really happening. In truth I was a bit miffed that I had been given the green light, the call to action, the big go-ahead, second-hand, like my importance to the scheme was flat zero. I might have felt more charitable had I known what a nightmare week it had been for those trusty co-conspirators of mine! But I would learn about it soon enough.

That night I was blissfully untroubled, well down the track at my local watering hole, when the barman shouted that there was a telephone call for Hayden.

"What are you doing down there!" snapped the Phantom. "You're supposed to be up here!"

"Well, what the hell do you think I am? A bloody mind-reader?"

"Get your arse up here right away!" he demanded, and hung up.

"Get stuffed!" I shouted into the dead line, and went back to the bar, my blood up. I had earnestly tried to stop the ring-in, I had offered a good alternative plan, I had floated Fine Cotton twice and saddled him at three meetings, and I had been conned into fronting as trainer on the day. But I was not going to interrupt good drinking time to be at Gillespie's beck and call if he took that tone of voice. I was going to get good and tight, and rethink the whole involvement in the morning.

The telephone rang at four in the morning, and this time John was really agitated.

"Hayden? Why haven't you left yet? I've been waiting all night!"

"Well, to tell you the truth I'd like to get an idea what's going on," I replied, "so you better fill me in or I'm not moving."

"Yeah, righto. I'll put it this way. You ever heard of a bloke called Silvertongue?"

"No. What's he got to do with it?"

"He's here in Brisbane as a watchdog for all the people putting money into this, and I can tell you he's been bloody heavy about it, especially when it didn't come off last week. He's a nice enough sort of bloke but I don't want to push him, see? He wants you up in Brisbane."

"That's your problem," I yawned.

Gillespie paused.

"It's just he knows who you are, and he knows that your brother is riding at Southport tomorrow, so he reckons there'll be a couple of boys to keep an eye on him down there. If I were you, I'd get up here."

"Pat?"

The Phantom's voice turned gentle.

"That's not my fault, Hayden, but we need you now. Okay?"

For a moment there was silence, then the line clicked dead.

I lay in my bed and reflected. It was heavier than I thought, and I vaguely recalled hearing something about an internationally famous con nicknamed Silvertongue. Gillespie was probably genuine, but if this heavy thought he could put the weights on me by mentioning Pat he was wrong, because Pat could take care of himself better than they realised. I fell asleep, thinking what a silly thing it was to be called Silvertongue.

I woke at dawn and took my horses down for their morning work. Perhaps I sensed it was the last I would train because I took it easy, taking time to enjoy the chill, the scents, the smooth feel of the stopwatch, the hard drum of hooves, the track riders' casual obscenities, the steam rising from the horses' flanks in the grey, early light.

I found Bobby North's place in Brisbane late that afternoon, steeling myself for a dressing-down from the Phantom, but hoping to get a few things straight with this Silvertongue character. I had rehearsed my lines in the car and strode down the manicured path to the house with my jaw set.

"Oh, there you are, Haitch!" Gillespie said brightly. "I was wondering when you'd turn up. Bobby's gone to the gym and John Dixon is with the horse. Like a beer?"

"Too right! Is that Silvertongue here?"

"No. He's staying in town and said he had to make a few calls."

"And he's pretty heavy, eh?"

"Well, I don't know about him, but I know his connections are. You should have seen his face when I told him the ring-in was off last week! He nearly exploded!"

"Yes, what happened about that?"

Gillespie busied himself with beer in North's spotless kitchen, carefully wiping rings of condensation from the bench.

"Tell you the truth I didn't work up the courage to tell anyone until the Thursday night, when Bobby and Silvertongue turned up. We were at this pub having a few drinks and Silvertongue—he's a super-smoothie, smoked salmon sort — he's preening away and Bobby is bubbling on the way he does and I thought I'd hit them with it when they were in a good mood. I just told them there was a problem and they looked at me like they hoped it wasn't serious and I told them straight out. Well, Silvertongue gulps what's left in his glass and Bobby goes all dark and everyone just sits there. So I asked Silvertongue what he thinks and he tells me I've got to get on the 'phone straight away. I said I wasn't going to do it so it better be him."

"How did he take that?" I asked, admiring John's gall.

"It was funny. He takes off for the 'phone but I saw him stop at the bar for a quick slug on the way. When he got back he said they wanted to talk to me, so I went over and this fellow read me the riot act. I just said that if they wanted to get heavy so could we, and not to worry, that everything would be all right for next week, which is tomorrow."

"What about that? Did you find another horse?"

"Yes, we did. That's a funny story too. Just wait on while I crack another bottle."

I pulled my chair in for John to squeeze past and smiled at the thought of Silvertongue getting all panicky while Gillespie was so cool. It was supposed to be the other way around, in theory. The Phantom returned with froth on his lips, already into the story.

". . . so when Dashing Soltaire came fourth to him, I thought this horse might be useful in the future. Name's Bold Personality, owned by a trainer called Bill Naoum, down Ballina way. Nice bloke and a top trainer too, but he drives a hard bargain. He wanted twenty grand for him, and like Bobby said that time, we didn't have the cash."

"I take it this is the new ring-in?"

"Bold Personality? That's right. You know the horse?"

"I might have heard of him, but I don't remember what he looks like."

"Mmm. So we had to work out some way to get hold of him. So I called Bill and said there was a Chinese syndicate interested and I'd be sending a bloke down — that was Dixon — who could write him a cheque on the spot. But I said not to cash it until Monday, when the Chinese money would be through. That way we could either use the money we won on the ring-in to pay for it, or take it back and say we'd lost interest."

"And did Naoum fall for it?"

"What happened was this. Twenty grand was top money for the horse so he was prepared to wear it for the time being. The funny bit is—you know how I told you John Dixon knows nothing about horses? Well, we had to wait until yesterday to send him down, so Bill's got less time to check up on it. The first thing John Dixon knows he has to leave here straight away to drive down to Ballina and pick up the horse. So he grabs this mate of his and they're just about to leave and he says 'What about a float?' I said to go hire one, but it's show week and they were all out except this tiny, rickety thing, so they grab that and hightail it."

"And Naoum took the cheque?"

"Yes, but wait on. It gets better. When they get there, old Bill thinks he's got to do a good sales job on Dixon and Dixon thinks he's got to do a good con job on Bill. So they parade around and around the horse with Johnny making stupid comments about this leg and that rump, and Bill wondering what the hell is going on. When he's finally written the cheque and they go to load Personality on the float it's too small for him. Dixon says something clever like 'It doesn't fit!'."

"You're making this up!"

"No! It's true! So suddenly Dixon's got the whole ring-in riding on him and he doesn't know what to do. Then Bill offers to take it up to Brisbane today, because he's got a double float and one of his own horses is running two races after ours tomorrow, so he . . ."

"Hang on!" I said, suddenly alert. "So Naoum is going to be at Eagle Farm tomorrow?"

"Well, he actually had Bold Personality entered. He's running something else instead."

"Oh, Johnny!"

"What?"

"Do you mean to say that our ring-in was already entered for tomorrow? That we're taking him out of one race and running him as Fine Cotton in another? With his owner on course?"

"Yes, but who's going to know?"

"Is he close to Fine Cotton? They'd want to be twins!"

"Ahh. Well, he's got good speed. He'll win it easy, especially if you've got that bomb you were talking about.'

"But do they look the same?"

"Well, like you said. It's a—what was it?"

"Mortal lock?"

"Yes. A mortal lock. That's good, that. He's the wrong age and he's the wrong colour but no-one is going to be looking. How's your beer?"

"Dead!" I said, with feeling.

Gillespie rose, and this time I didn't shift my chair. He went the long way through the lounge for another bottle, raising his voice so I could hear.

"Anyway, the long and the short of it is we put Bill's 'phone out of order by calling up from a public box and leaving our end off the hook so he couldn't check with the bank, and Dixon picked Personality up today."

It was about our eighth bottle. I was starting to feel a little light headed.

"You crazy bastard, Gillespie! Every jockey worth his salt will see that our Fine Cotton is the wrong colour! What colour is he?"

"He's a brown. But we're going to dye him darker tonight. That's another funny story."

"Is there more?"

"You'll love this," said the Phantom, overfilling my glass. "See, you dye horses with that hair stuff that women use."

"Can you do that? Have you ever done it?"

"Yeah, I've done it lots of times. You shampoo it in. It's easy. But anyway, Bob and I hunt around till we find a chemist and I say, 'Five tubes of that' and this woman says, 'But madame will only need one. It will last her for weeks!' She kept insisting, so we're worried about raising suspicion and we had to drive all over town to get enough for the job!"

"Incredible!"

The Phantom studied me carefully for sarcasm, and found what he was looking for. With his eyes fixed on me he leaned down beside his chair and resurfaced with a sheet of paper.

"See this? Papers for the ring-in," he said, "with Fine Cotton's name and Bold Personality's description. Expert forgery."

He handed the sheet over. I gave it the once-over and it looked good.

"That's a coincidence, though," I said, genuinely surprised. "Bold Personality's got white socks on the back like Cotton."

"Yeah, that's a bit of a worry, because he hasn't. That was a mistake. I was thinking of painting some on." He shrugged. "But these are just for emergencies, because the stewards and cops we need are on side, like I said."

I had meant to talk to the Phantom about that. I tipped the dregs of the beer into my glass.

"Look, exactly what is the story there? Who's with us, exactly?"

"You know how it is, Hayden," said Gillespie sincerely. "I don't like to dob, so let's just say that business has been done on a few favours, some up-front cash and a lot of promises."

Gillespie stood and collected the empty beer bottles and glasses.

I followed him into the kitchen. "But wasn't it risky to set up? And you still wouldn't know if a cop or a steward was planning to doublecross us! They could be pretending to go along for the moment, to give us enough rope to hang ourselves."

"They'd be hanging all their mates as well, or be pretty unpopular at the least. A lot of highly placed people have plans to make a nest egg on this one. And who wins points by doing a boss out of his dough? I tell you, Hayden, we could run a purple horse tomorrow and no one would notice. It's home and hosed."

"Yes, if Bold Personality wins, that is."

The Phantom extracted a set of keys from his pocket and smiled.

"That's your problem. Come on, John Dixon will be wondering what the hell has happened to us. We still have to colour in that horse."

Both of us were talked out and drove in silence to stables on the outskirts of Brisbane where both Fine Cotton and the ring-in were stashed. It was late and John Dixon, a big man with coiffed hair and a huge, blonde moustache, was clearly relieved to see us.

We were shaking hands when I caught my first glimpse of what had to be Bold Personality, and I went straight into shock. He looked nothing like Fine Cotton, and broad sweat stains streaked his flanks. I turned on poor Dixon like a yellow dog.

"What have you done?"

"What do you mean?" he said, surprised by the tone. "I only brought him here."

"With this on?" I raised the corner of a heavy winter rug.

"That's right."

"No, that's wrong!"

The rug was far too heavy for the conditions. Bold Personality was lathered in sweat, and badly dehydrated.

"He won't run like this," I warned, and turned to Gillespie. "You'd know that, John. He's lost all his essential salts."

"Shit, really?" said Dixon.

"Look, don't worry about it for now," Gillespie said. "We'll drench him later and get the salts back in, but now we better get on with this dyeing."

It must have looked awfully funny, because it felt very bloody undignified—three cons at the heart of a dark plot to take the bookies for a fortune, on the eve of the big sting, in green dishwashing gloves, up to our elbows in dark brown bubbles. But we worked with a will and Bold Personality was a very sorry horse, thoroughly hosed and shampooed, when we stood back to survey the job. It was pitch black outside and we were under yellowish stable lights so it was difficult to see how well the dye had taken or exactly what colour we had ended up with, but he looked as though he'd pass, and the Phantom pronounced it a success.

I was against the drenching because I think it's a vet's job, especially if you're rushed and in poor light. The object is to get a special liquid into the animal—a mixture which restores the salts to a natural balance—but you have to run a tube through its nose and right down into its stomach to do it. Horses dislike it and get restless, meaning that you can end up pumping fluid into the lungs. I wasn't going to be responsible for that.

"Sorry, Johnny, no way," I said firmly. "If you want to drench him, you do it. I'll be over saying hello to Cotton."

"All right, Hayden, if that's what you reckon. I'll get some outside help."

When Gillespie's help arrived I was having a quiet chat with Fine Cotton, feeding him hay as he snuffled recognition. Not two minutes later the peace was shattered by a whinny of panic from Personality and a chorus of obscenities from the crew. The Phantom's outside assistance was an ordinary stablehand, who had just broken a blood vessel in the horse's nose. With great spurts it was Personality doing the drenching, spraying Dixon and Gillespie with crimson. They were frantic, and for a while, to make a point, I did nothing to help.

A bit of bleeding doesn't do a horse any harm, but it had to be stopped before he lost too much or he certainly wouldn't race tomorrow. Dixon was beside himself, and the Phantom was chanting: "Don't tell anybody! Don't tell anyone!" I couldn't bear to watch it any longer and stepped in. We tied a rope around Personality's neck and threw it up over the rafters to elevate his head, packed his nose in cold towels, and after a few minutes the bleeding slowed, then stopped. The drench was administered without further fuss, and Bold Personality was put to bed — very tired and emotional.

Gillespie, John Dixon and I drank on into the early hours, discussing our plans after the ring-in. The Phantom was visionary that night, painting pictures of a glorious team which would take the racing industry by storm with hit after hit, until it was conned into bankrupt submission. It was an inspired sell, one of his best, because Dixon and I waved our drunken farewells with unbounded enthusiasm for the sting, and complete confidence in its success.

Chapter Eighteen
DIXON

The dawn of 18 August 1984 was brisk, bright and magical, under a clear blue Queensland winter's sky. It was a day for positive thinking, the sort of day nothing could go wrong with—if Gillespie had his stewards and cops on side as he was claiming. We had an entire morning to run through the plans and get the sequences straight, and such matters to discuss as how much cash was coming my way. They were all very pleasant thoughts and the day started well, but it deteriorated fast.

I got to Bobby North's house about 9 a.m., and even then calls were coming in ceaselessly from all over Australia.

"All Silvertongue's boys," confided the Phantom. "Betting agents, staked out everywhere you can lay it."

The telephone jangled again and without introduction Gillespie fired a message.

"She's right, mate. Everything's go."

He hung up. The telephone rang again immediately and it was a while before I got another word in.

"Who's picking up the horse?" I asked.

Gillespie folded his arms and looked around vaguely. "Sorry? Yes. You. Dixon will be here in a moment. Take his car."

"And the float. What are we doing for a float?"

"Yeah, there's a float," said the Phantom with supreme disinterest, "but you'll have to pick it up from the Gold Coast."

My blood ran cold.

"You'll have to step on it," he added.

John Dixon walked in then, shouting hellos, also unaware of the assignment, and equally shocked when he found out.

"I've only got a four cylinder. Will that tow a float and two horses?"

Gillespie sounded flustered. "Just get down the Coast and back as fast as you can!"

"These guys are idiots!" said Dixon, as we spun away from the curb in his little silver car.

"Don't worry, we won't pull the float, let alone two horses."

"You know Gillespie says we're off the planet unless this thing comes off?" said Dixon, racing through the gears.

"I think he might be having you on, but I'd like to know more about this Silvertongue cove."

"I know he acts as a pipeline for whoever is backing us. It took a fair bit of money to set the thing up. Gillespie says the heavies have made Silvertongue personally responsible for bringing this thing off no matter what. He's got a gun. I know that much."

"I'll tell you something, Johnny. The way it looks to me, you'd think these guys actually wanted this thing to fall in a heap."

Dixon and I looked at each other in sudden surprise. Without thinking, I had voiced one hell of a subconscious doubt — the possibility of a doublecross.

"Why do you say that?"

"I don't know. Maybe because it looks so unprofessional, like the Phantom isn't really trying. And maybe because we're taking his word for so much. It's nothing I know for sure, but now I think about it, it's worth keeping your eyes open. I wouldn't put it past him."

Dixon drove in silence for another few miles, his brain working as hard as the car.

"But how could Gillespie gain from a doublecross?"

"What about through the bookies? The only people who stand to make money by exposing the ring-in are bookies. First they'd have to take every bet they could grab on Fine Cotton — Silvertongue's plunge and the rest — then call foul after the race was run. The horse is disqualified and they get to keep all the bets that way. It's risky, though. If anything went wrong they'd have to pay out. Maybe Gillespie has got a few bob each way."

"I don't think he'd do that though, do you?" asked Dixon, lamely.

It was treasonous talk, and we each decided to leave it pretty much at that.

I changed the subject: "What's your background anyway, John?"
"I was a cop."
"Really? What made you swap sides?"
"Do you really want my life story?" asked Dixon, doubtfully.
"Sure. No, really. I really do."

I ripped the ring-pull from a can of beer, and John Dixon started up. Something more than twenty years ago he had come over from Britain as a lad involved in something called the "Big Brother" scheme. This scheme provided fares to Australia for Britain's young unemployed, and guaranteed farm work once they got here. It sounded fine to Dixon, but when he fronted at his assigned farm he found out he had been hired as a dog.

"My job was to herd sheep," he said, his voice offended. "I rode with the dogs, was whistled at like a dog, lived in a dirt floor lean-to like a dog and they actually treated me like a dog. I couldn't cut that much charity, so I bolted for Melbourne."

For years in Melbourne Dixon lived under bridges and off the streets, with doorstep milk money his main source of income.

"Eventually I got a job as an apprentice metal worker, but I borrowed heaps of copper sheeting to sell for entertainment money, and I had to bolt when the scam came undone."

Dixon cut cane in Cairns, and off-season he worked as a rigger. He says that was the last time he ever really worried about anything.

"I was walking the streets looking for work when I happened on this construction site. The foreman said his rigger hadn't turned up and I could give it a shot if I had the guts — all I had to do was ride a steel girder five floors up in the air and bolt it in. He gave me the tools and I got onto this big length of steel, but when they craned me up, I froze. I couldn't move, and the bastards just laughed. They left me up there half the day, and when they got me down I really wanted to kill someone. But the foreman said to come back the next day and it would be different. And it was, too. I couldn't give a damn about heights anymore and worked there for ages. It just shows there's no point getting upset."

After a brief return trip to England, where he married, Dixon returned to Australia looking for security. He applied to join the Victorian police force, was accepted, and had managed to finish most of his training when the Department discovered he had a conviction for car theft. That made him ineligible, but he tried for a special clearance.

"I got it just in time, because the chief who gave it to me was drummed out of the force for corruption a few weeks later."

Johnny Dixon trod the beat for a few years, gradually becoming disenchanted with the dull sameness of the job, until one night a seemingly trivial incident changed his life.

"I was on point duty, bored as hell, when this bloke skids to a stop in a new Cadillac. I left the traffic to itself and walked over close because I was fascinated by this car. The driver was a little fat bloke who didn't look like much, and when I asked him, politely enough, how he managed to afford a car like that he looked at me like I was scum and said, 'Not by doing what you're doing'. When I thought about it, it made a lot of sense."

"I applied to join the police force once," I said. "I was crooked enough, but not tall enough."

"Well, see, I was the other way around! So anyway, after that I got into door-to-door sales and did pretty well, mostly up in Queensland with a pool outfit. Then I met Bobby North and went into selling paint jobs for him, and now this. Now I'm up to my arse in crocodiles with Gillespie, just like you."

When we reached the Gold Coast the float was ready, but we were late as hell and reduced to a crawl with it in tow. We had yet to pick up the horses in Brisbane and time was of the essence, in more respects than one, because I had to make a difficult decision.

The events of last night were a problem. I wasn't at all confident that Personality could win against the novices—not after being bled and dyed and kept up so late—unless I gave him the bomb. The only way I could guarantee the win was a full needle of the stuff, but in that case my last-minute emergency plan would go down the spout, because no matter what Gillespie said, I had not given up on the idea of running the real Fine Cotton with the bomb.

Just before we left the stables on Friday night, I had convinced him that we should take both horses to the track, to swap them back straight after the race in case there was any delayed trouble. But the strategy was really for my own purpose. If the scam was looking too last-minute fragile, I could always pull a double switch. The trouble was that when I made this plan I thought Personality could win without dope. Now my opinion had changed. I only had one dose, it had to be administered well beforehand and the deadline was approaching. Whichever horse took the full load was the one I would be committed to race. My own instincts screamed "Fine Cotton" but I knew that for me there would be awful hell to pay if he failed to take first for any unlikely reason.

I agonised in the dim hush of the stable, collecting both horses, and walking them into the yard. We ambled over to where John Dixon waited by the ramp of the double float, and straight away I was sure that something was wrong. It was in John Dixon's face. Following his eyeline, I turned around to where Bold Personality shone brilliantly in the bright daylight.

"Will you look at that," he said softly. "The fucking horse is red." And so he was. Not a burgundy nor a maroon kind of red, but a gaudy, glossy bright red. He looked ridiculous.

"Oh well, that's it!" said Dixon. "We'll all head for the hills and let someone put this scam out of its misery. I better call Bob and tell him to can it."

I followed him to the office, hearing his end of the telephone call as if it came from far away. I didn't have to listen to know what the outcome would be.

"Still on," he said flatly. "Gillespie just got off the phone to Silvertongue who says he can't stop the plunge. It's got to go ahead. Silvertongue's on his way to Bob's now."

"What do you think he'll say when he sees a red horse? I know for a fact this one won't pass inspection."

"I said the same, but Gillespie said you could run a purple horse today because no one's looking."

"He keeps saying that!"

"Anyway, they want the horses at Bob's place as soon as possible."

"Just a moment, Dicky. This won't take a sec."

Needle in hand, I looked at the two contrasting rumps.

Bold Personality was undeniably red, and whether the stewards were lined up or not, I couldn't believe they'd let the Phantom go that far. All it would take to force an inquiry was one track professional who knew damn well that Fine Cotton was black, and then all of us, bar the bookies, were down the drain. All of us except the bookies, and maybe, just maybe, the Phantom. It was strictly hunch territory now, and on sheer gut feeling, I raised the needle over the bay.

"Another thing Gillespie says is that they'll have us under surveillance at the track," said Dixon. "I don't like the sound of that."

I lowered the needle. Surveillance could throw my timing out to buggery. It would be bloody hard to pull a double switch with the Phantom's associates crowding the wings, whoever they were. And if I couldn't pull the switch, poor Personality could be racing without the bomb. It made the decision still harder.

"Who's going to be watching us?"

"Silvertongue's crowd. But I suppose we can't go far wrong if we just do as we're told."

In an instant, without thought, just to get it over with, on a whim, I plunged home the "patent Haitana bomb".

Chapter Nineteen
SILVERTONGUE

Dixon's tiny car made a liar of me by struggling up Bobby North's driveway with the float in tow, as a tall, distinguished-looking gentleman walked from the back door of the house to meet us.

"Silvertongue," groaned Dixon. "Just wait till he sees this!"

There were no introductions. We went straight to work, lowering the ramp and bringing Fine Cotton out first.

"What's this one?" asked Silvertongue in a pleasant bass. "It's not the ring-in, surely!"

"No, that's Fine Cotton," Dixon said.

"I was about to say! He's got no condition on him."

"This is the ring-in," I said as I backed Personality into the sunshine. "Bold Personality, alias Fine Cotton. What do you think?"

It was almost impossible to keep the smile off my face because Dixon was doubled up with laughter behind the float where Silvertongue couldn't see him. When I trusted myself to face our gentlemanly heavy it was worse because the face was priceless. His eyes and mouth were wide and strange small noises were coming from deep down in his throat. I left him alone in his misery to pop upstairs, grab a beer, and see what was to be done. I could hear the telephone still running hot.

And the comedy continued indoors. The Phantom was sitting at the verandah table, his ear glued to the phone, staring at the horse and making a valiant attempt to sound confident.

"Yep. She's . . . ah . . . all right!" he stammered, then mouthed something at me which I couldn't quite make out.

His mouth opened like he was grinning then went into a pursed "O" shape. It was far too much and I burst into laughter, making Gillespie go dark.

"Sham-bloody-poo!" he shouted when he put down the telephone, and it was all hands on deck.

Silvertongue was pacing with one hand clasped behind his neck, long-faced, chain-smoking, watching Gillespie, Dixon and me up to our arms in red foam, scrubbing poor, bewildered Personality. I stopped for a moment to cheer him up.

"Don't worry, mate. He'll be the cleanest horse in town! We'll win a prize with him."

"Shut up! Just shut up!"

He looked so incredibly miserable that I just had to break up again and everyone else started laughing along. A carnival atmosphere had taken all of us, and even Silvertongue forced a grin.

"Now, tell me once again, will you John? Nobody, and I mean nobody, is going to inspect this animal. Correct?" Silvertongue asked.

"That's right, Jack. You tell him, Hayden."

"If I thought somebody was going to check this horse I'd have made my own bloody plans by now!" I laughed.

Silvertongue, or Jack as the Phantom called him, struggled through another rueful grin.

'You chaps are beyond the pale. Just like your horse, I might add. Bloody hell!"

But Bold Personality was returning to his original colour, and out came the booze in celebration. Parties of two and three people I didn't know were coming in at intervals to watch the proceedings, and I supposed they had something to do with Silvertongue or Gillespie, because no one seemed to mind. From then on it was like a Saturday morning working bee, casual and good-humoured, and once again I had to admire the Phantom's style. He spoke to our pistol-packing guard like they were old mates and I could see Silvertongue responding, becoming good-hearted, rather than the threatening heavy John Dixon had painted. The performance was classic Gillespie. Within a few hours Silvertongue would be taking orders without question like the rest of us, taking on responsibility which would gradually ease him into the scam until he was a key member of our side. That way, if it went wrong, he would be more likely to run for cover himself than to extract any kind of revenge. The Phantom took time to wink at me as we scrubbed, and blow me if I wasn't feeling invincible too.

The booze took hold and the work slowed, but then we weren't much conscious of deadline—not until Bobby North appeared from nowhere. He spiked any illusion of quiet confidence with one long stinger of a sentence, put straight to Silvertongue.

"Listen, you can see how bloody stupid this is. Why don't you get hold of your punters somehow and tell them this is a no show. I don't care who is on side. Something is going to stuff up somewhere. Forget it!"

In a matter of moments, Silvertongue's face seemed to have gone tiredly grey, and his shoulders slumped. He spoke in a flat, cultured monotone.

"Robert, there is nothing I'd like more, but I'm afraid it's out of the question. There are no ways out and no excuses, and I promise you that that goes for me too. So," he brightened, "all of you, just get on with it."

I wasn't sure about my timing, but someone had to say it: "Ahh . . . there's another little problem we might have to think about."

They each stared at me, Dixon with a slight grin, North and Silvertongue with glittering intensity, and the Phantom rolling his eyes. I let the silence hang.

"Well, what is it?" Silvertongue asked.

"Personality still has his work shoes on. There won't be time to get him fitted with racing plates, unless we leave now."

Eyes darted to watches, and the magnitude of our problem hit home. It was about eleven, and even forgetting the shoes, the latest we could be on course was just after one.

Silvertongue snapped icily: "Then for God's sake get dressed and get going!"

"We can't really," said Gillespie calmly, "because we've still got to paint those white socks on him and a track farrier would pick that up for sure."

I opened my mouth to speak—it would be simplest to bandage his hind legs and Gillespie must have known that—but he raised his hand.

"The farrier not on your payroll, John?" Silvertongue asked Gillespie with a hint of sarcasm.

"No. We'll have to get someone to come out here. I know a bloke who will probably do it."

"Well, get him!" snapped Silvertongue, one hand clasped behind his neck again, the tip of his cigarette glowing super-hot.

The Phantom glanced at his watch and hurried for the telephone, John Dixon excused himself to go home and get dressed, I opened another stubby, Silvertongue opened another packet of cigarettes and Bold Personality shone, his coat glowing with red highlights.

Just over an hour before deadline the blacksmith arrived with his gear, in no special hurry, and Gillespie was reluctant to tell him the job was urgent. The farrier was obviously suspicious, shooting pointed looks at streaks of red on the grass.

It was most unusual to be asked to come to a private home on race day, but a stubby slapped into his hand forestalled any questions. He drained it in two long swigs.

"We're just doing this for a friend, like," explained the Phantom, smooth as always, handing the blacksmith another beer.

The three of us stood in Bob North's backyard and chewed the fat, speaking of shared friends and exchanging track gossip. I noticed with amusement how the verandah curtains kept parting and closing as Bobby became frantic. When Gillespie went up to the house to grab a few more stubbies he had exploded.

"Look at the time! For Christ's sake stop feeding him stubbies. Just get the job done and piss him off!"

I brought Bold Personality out of North's garage and had another quick word with the farrier to make sure he did the job right.

"And what's his name?" the nuggety little fellow asked, his eyes narrowed.

"Fine Cotton. Why?"

"Yeah, that's what that smoothie said a moment ago. It's just that Gillespie said it was called something else."

"Oh, he's got it messed up. That's probably another one we've got running today."

"I see. Now, listen, I've only got these big-headed nails I usually use for trotters. They're going to stick out the bottom and give him running spikes. Is that a worry with the stewards? Should I get some shorter ones sent over?"

We should have. It was just another detail to go wrong, but it was too late.

"No, don't worry about it. He's going to need all the help he can get if you ask me. Can we get a move on? Time's short."

"How's it going, Hayden?" asked Gillespie, offering a fresh stubby.

"No worries. We're just getting into it now."

The farrier took a pull at his drink and winked at me. "Hey, John, what did you say the name of this one was?"

The Phantom looked him squarely in the eye, trapped. "Fine Cotton. I told you that other name because he's a hotty for Eagle Farm this arvo. That's why we're in a bit of a hurry."

The blacksmith did what every red-blooded Australian would do. He pulled a crumpled ten dollar note from his pocket and stuffed it into the Phantom's hand.

"I don't know what's going on here, mate," he said cautiously, "but this is a beautiful-looking animal. Anyone who can get a horse polished up like this has got to know what he's doing. You put this on for me, hey?"

It's no wonder he was impressed. Personality was shining like a beacon, shampooed to within an inch of his life.

As the farrier got to work I took Gillespie aside. "You know we'd better get some racing plates on Fine Cotton, too. If he's dragged out for inspection sometime after the race they'll notice he's still wearing working shoes."

The Phantom gazed at me through narrowed eyes. "No, don't worry about it, Hayden. We'll say that's how he raced. Work shoes would have slowed him up if anything, so they can fine us but they can't say he didn't win fair and square."

The plates were fixed quickly and Gillespie hurried our friend down the driveway while I ducked into the house for a quick shower. A few minutes later I was towelling my hair, trying to struggle into a suit and drink a stubby at the same time when I heard a big commotion outside. I poked my head through a window to see Personality rearing up, Silvertongue holding him by the halter and the Phantom attacking his hind legs with a can of white spray paint.

"Stop it!" I shouted. "Stop that! When he hears that thing hiss he thinks it's a bloody snake! You'll get that paint all over him!"

When Personality calmed down, Gillespie stood up to survey his handiwork. Sticky white paint matted the hair, dribbling down onto his shoes.

"Give him some socks like Cotton," Gillespie said.

"That looks terrible!" moaned Silvertongue, examining the uneven mess of white.

"Leave it to me and I'll do something. Just a tick," I sighed, returning to the house for a tie.

A few minutes — that's all the time they were alone — and when I returned they had tried to wash the paint off with water, creating a gooey, soggy, oil-based mess. And still dissatisfied, Silvertongue was spraying the lot with brown paint to get his legs looking back to normal.

"That's somewhat worse," he said, and found no argument.

They sat back on their haunches and turned to me with raised eyebrows.

"Any ideas, Haitch?" asked the Phantom.

"Look, fellers. All we have to do is bandage it up. No one will be able to tell like that."

Silvertongue thought for a moment. "What about the vet? If he sees bandages, won't he want to know what's wrong with his legs?"

"He might, but it's a hell of a lot better than parading him around with paint all over him. It's the easiest, that's all."

"Should have thought of it in the first place," added the Phantom, avoiding my glare. "See what I told you, Jack? Hayden's a top bloke to have aboard!"

Time dribbled away as I stitched on the bandages, front and back, so that if there happened to be an inspection it was evens we'd sneak through.

When at last all was close to readiness we had less than forty minutes to drive across town, and to me it looked like we were buggered.

Silvertongue was hard on my back and his language had deteriorated.

"Just get the fuck out of here!" he shouted.

But there was one last thing to settle. "It's your scam, Johnny," I said to the Phantom. "You pick the racing colours."

I held out three sets of them, and without hesitation Gillespie grabbed a vest — a gold vest overlaid with five orange circles.

"You would!"

"What?"

"Those are my jail colours!"

"What?"

"Come on! Come on!" shouted Silvertongue, steel in his voice by now. "Move it! And listen, you chaps, I don't care how you do it but get there on time. Hayden, go with Dixon and I'll take your car. And remember, you'll be watched. Constantly. All of you!"

Dixon and I boarded his car with less than half an hour to make the track, and were all fired up and ready to go when Bobby North dashed from the house.

"Listen, you blokes, make sure we're not seen together at the track, okay? Just in case something goes wrong. And good luck!"

Dixon faced him resignedly.

"You're not coming, are you, Bob?"

"Don't worry, mate. I'll be there. I won't leave you posted. But I sure won't be backing Cotton."

As the engine raced, the clutch engaged and we kangaroo'd into the unknown, an off-key version of "Liberty Valance" started playing in my head.

Chapter Twenty
EAGLE FARM

"Well, what do you reckon?" I said brightly to Dixon as the gears ground.

"How would I know? I'm like you—in the bloody dark on these things."

"Gillespie would have to be pretty confident about these people at the track, wouldn't he?"

"Yes, I s'pose so."

"Then why do you think he took those fake papers away from me, just before we left?"

"You're joking! What if they ask for them?"

"That's what I mean. He'd either have to be pretty confident or this is a set up."

Dixon hit a pothole and the car kangaroo'd for half the next block.

"What worries me is that Bob wanted to can it. I've known him for a long time and he's a stickler for detail. You've only got to look at his house and garden. Trims his lawn with nail scissors. He'd know what the odds are and he's not too happy."

"It's a bit late now, isn't it?"

"That's right. He was so enthusiastic when we got into this thing in the first place. He called me over one day and said we were out of paint and into ring-ins. I didn't even know what a ring-in was, but everything he's touched has turned to gold so I couldn't see any reason why I shouldn't be in."

"You don't think Bobby's in with Gillespie, pulling some sort of stunt on us, do you?"

Dixon looked genuinely surprised.

"No way. No, I don't know what Gillespie's up to but I know Bob's solid. It's more likely that Silvertongue. It's him if it's anyone."

"But did you see the Phantom do the job on him this morning? He ended up trying to paint the horse's feet himself! No, I think Gillespie's style would be to go with someone right outside our circle."

Dixon pulled up at a set of lights, cursing the delay, but it gave him an idea.

"What if we got a flat tyre? They couldn't blame us for that, could they? And then we'd be too late!"

I rolled my eyes. It was the oldest and worst excuse imaginable. I tried to offer comfort.

"Well, we've got to be on course an hour in advance to pay for the entry. We're late now, and we're moving at just over bloody walking speed so they'll probably scratch it anyway."

"And what happens then? Are we all in for a bullet?"

"I honestly doubt it. Like you said, how can they blame you and me? It's not our idea. We've done what they asked."

Dixon brightened. He suggested that we drive even more slowly, but if we were under surveillance and it looked like we were stalling it could buy us trouble. We compromised by steering into every pothole we could spot but the little car wouldn't give up.

"You know we're gone, don't you?" said Dixon with finality. "I mean it's all right for me, but racing is your game."

"There's nothing to do. I've tried everything apart from going to the cops and if they're on side with the Phantom, what hope have we got?"

"No, wait on, Hayden," he said. "We've got the real Fine Cotton in the back there. Do you reckon he's got a chance? What if we raced him instead?"

"There's hope for you yet, Johnny. You know that needle I gave Cotton this morning? It's my own undetectable dope. If we can get through Silvertongue's coast-watchers and pull a double switch he's going to romp home."

"Oh, brilliant!"

"The only worry is he's still got working shoes on, but if the Phantom's stewards are playing blind, what the hell? If they pick it up and disqualify him before the start, we'll know we were done anyway. And the way he's charged up he'll win, working shoes or not."

"Well, that's fantastic, Hayden! What a bloody relief!"

But we weren't home yet, merely approaching the first checkpoint at Eagle Farm. It was the float gate, where horses are counted off and stall numbers allocated, and a white-coated attendant rose from a deck chair to meet us.

"You stay in the car," I said, "and I'll get out to distract him. When I give you the signal, come straight through and don't stop."

"What if he does stop me?"

"Put it this way. If we can't even get through the front gate, we haven't got much hope have we? We'll go home!"

Without waiting for a reply I sprang from the car and strode purposefully toward the attendant. "I've got Fine Cotton on board, race four. What's his stall number and where can we park?"

I waved frantically behind my back, but the car stayed where it was. I waved harder, but by then the gatekeeper was on his way over for a look. I caught Dixon's eye and he shrugged.

"What about this other?"

"A scratching," I replied, "coming straight back out."

"All right. Thank you. Through you go, now."

It was an extra hot performance and I was elated.

"Get cold feet, did you?" I said to Dixon. "There's nothing to worry about!" I laughed as I caught up with the car—and somewhere in the sky, the great gods of chance smiled their secret smiles.

Bang! Bang! BANG! Dixon was half out of his seat and my heart was pounding like a pile-driver!

"Jesus!" sweated Dixon. "Was that the horse?"

Fine Cotton let loose with another couple of giant kicks and the whole float shook.

"That's the bomb starting to work. Listen, the coast looks clear over here. I'll get him out before he kicks it to bloody matchwood."

"So, we're going with Cotton?"

"You bloody bet!"

"You bloody ripper!"

I lowered the ramp and backed the bay out, with something dragging my eyes downward, something wrong. For a moment my eyes refused to believe what they saw, and then I had my weight into his rump, fiercely shoving him back into the float and pulling Bold Personality out instead. Fine Cotton let out a great whinny and Dixon was craning his head from the driver's window.

"What? Personality? Has someone spotted us?"

"You won't believe it. One of those kicks has bent a back shoe. He can't run! Oh, shit and bugger it!"

I snatched my gear from the rear seat.

"What are you going to do?" asked Dixon, as though it didn't matter. Silently I shouldered the equipment and led Bold Personality away toward his stall.

"Goodbye, you poor bastard," he said after me.

I turned back and our eyes locked. "This is it, mate. I'm gone."

I felt strangely calm about it, luckily, because my composure was in for another solid shaking only moments afterward.

"Hayden Haitana, report to the Stewards Office!" the public address system boomed.

"Aarrgh!" I shuddered, and then suddenly someone had me by the shoulder with enough grip to spin me right around. I feared the worst but it was just another trainer.

"Your horse is losing a bandage, mate."

"What? Which?" I almost shouted at him.

Startled, he stared at me as I slowly turned, expecting to see a mess of paint and matted hair, but it was a front leg. I found myself laughing with relief and clapped the trainer a little too hard on the shoulder.

"Thanks, mate. I could've had trouble with the stewards on that one!"

I put Personality in his stall and repaired the bandage, then bubbled over to the main office. I bubbled because by then I honestly couldn't give a stuff. I had no idea why they wanted me and could only assume that someone had heard something on the grapevine, because it's almost impossible to keep plans for a plunge under wraps. If they had, big deal. I would find the Phantom and fill him in and he would simply tell me to go ahead as planned.

My own last chance to intervene was up in smoke and I was going to take it as it came. Nothing was going to ruin the adventure. This was the big time, and especially interesting because there were so many factors at work and so much at stake. I was locked in, and once resigned, very much enjoying it!

"Mr Haitana," said the Chief Steward, "you have failed to declare your jockey for Fine Cotton in the fourth."

What jockey? On Gillespie's instructions I had offered a friend of mine ten thousand dollars to ride Cotton, but when the money didn't come through I had told him to forget it. The Phantom said he was going to book someone else.

"You've done this before," the steward said. "What's your excuse?"

"No excuse, sir," I said, resisting the urge to giggle.

"This misdemeanour carries a twenty-dollar fine. Pay the office clerk."

I strolled back to the stalls for my money and returned whistling to the members' stand where the fine was to be paid.

"No, mate," said the attendant, "you'll have to have a jacket to get in here."

"But I'm a trainer!" I protested. "I only want to pay a bloody fine!"

"Rules are rules."

"You mean fools are fools!" I muttered, and when I came back wearing the jacket the attendant was snaky as hell because he had heard my parting shot.

"You know you'll need a tie to get in here, don't you."

"Hell's bells!" I said. "I hope you're not this tough with your horses!"

Once I was dressed well enough to pay the fine I was running short of time, but back at the stalls I discovered that Gillespie had hired a strapper to assist me. It was just like him — she was gorgeous, innocent as a rose, good at her job, blissfully ignorant and a big plus to our operation. No one would suspect this girl of anything, and it would be she who took Personality through three separate stewards' checks. When the time came for her to saddle up I had a quick chat with a jockey the Phantom had hired at the last moment, and then we were underway.

The first check was crucial — at the mounting yard, where brands and markings are supposed to be matched against the horse's papers. In our case the stewards were going to find it difficult, as we had no papers to show them. It was the point of no return. If Personality's identity was questioned there I could plead stupidity and have a go at getting off, but once he was through it was fraud. I clenched my fists and gave them a good, gleeful shake as he walked past the stewards, all with their backs to him. As easily as that, Bold Personality had officially become Fine Cotton.

From then on it was a coast. His racing plates were supposed to be checked and he could have been disqualified for having the running spikes, but there was no inspection. Any horse sporting bandages should be given the once-over to see that they're properly stitched on, but again, no check. He was paraded for the punters looking an absolute picture, his head up, dancing around the enclosure, and my heart went out to him. The poor animal had been carted all over the place, dehydrated, dyed, bled, drenched, kept up late, and now he was to run this particular distance for the first time in his life.

"I doubt he'll have the stamina for it today," I said to the jockey as I legged him up, "so hold him back as long as possible, then give him his head and see what happens."

I could see the tote board from the mounting yard and noticed that Fine Cotton's odds had plummeted from 33-1 to 7-2. That indicated a huge on-course plunge, and now the jockeys were on to it. On their way to the barriers a huddle of them were bringing their horses up close to check him over.

"Madness," I said out loud, and turned my back on it.

I hurried off to the betting ring with twenty dollars to punt, and every cent of it was going on Harbour Gold. The betting ring was sheer bedlam. I struggled through the crowd to take Harbour Gold at 4-1 and the bookie was almost pathetically grateful.

"Hey, look at this!" he shouted to the crowd. "Here's someone who isn't taking Fine Cotton! Take a bloody bow, will you, mate?"

Cotton was the rage of the year, and some bookies were refusing to take any more bets on him. Others offered ridiculously poor odds, and even then, hands full of cash were thrust at them as fast as they could take it. The whole crowd was buzzing with the plunge, and the wizened old blokes with their pork pie hats and transistor radios nodded knowingly at each other. The whole thing stank to high heaven.

"Now, look, you blokes," the Phantom had said, "not a penny is to go on Cotton at Eagle Farm. We don't want to spark off a plunge and draw attention."

Attention? It was a riot!

Chapter Twenty-one
THE RACE

Fine Cotton delivered a succession of mighty kicks to the float and Dixon cringed. He was trying to lie low but it was becoming increasingly difficult as the "patent Haitana bomb" worked its magic on the horse. People were starting to look and in a moment he would have to take some kind of drastic action. He was still working on his options when Cotton loosed off another barrage, and Dixon found himself looking directly at the staring face of Bill Naoum. He had known Bill had a horse racing that day, but until that moment he hadn't realised the implications. If Naoum happened to see the race he would recognise his own horse for sure, and that would be the end of it. Dixon panicked, abandoning the car to lose himself in the crowd and to find the Phantom.

In the bedlam of the betting ring, Gillespie was unruffled.

"No sweat," he shouted. "Look, you take Cotton for a drive somewhere to settle him down and I'll look after Bill Naoum. Just make sure you get back after the race."

But Silvertongue, who was in on the conversation, was aghast.

"Bill Naoum? Here? But what if he sees his horse?"

"Don't worry about it, Jack. That's where you come in!"

The Phantom's plan was ingenious, if a little shaky. Silvertongue was to set up in the bar, posing as a southern buyer in Brisbane for the Winter Racing Carnival, while Gillespie convinced Naoum he had a sure sale on one of his other horses if he could just spare a moment for a drink with the prospect. Silvertongue's task was to keep Bill at the bar for as long as necessary—in spite of the fact that one of his horses was running two races after Cotton—and to make sure he was facing away from the race television monitor. Silvertongue was supposed to be a world-class con man, but the task was going to be bloody difficult.

Bobby North had arrived, running straight into his friend, Mally MacGregor Lowndes, whom the Phantom had set up as half-owner of Fine Cotton. Mally was a cagey old character. He had watched the prices on his horse crash, and was in a frightful dither because he knew Robert well enough to be sure that the plunge spelled capital C-O-N.

"What am I going to say, Robert? What am I going to say?" he moaned, wringing his hands.

"I don't know, Mally, but you better think of something quick. You've only got five minutes!"

"I know! I'll tell 'em I've taken sick! I'll ask 'em for a cuppa tea!"

With only moments before the start the Phantom had abandoned Silvertongue, talking bull in the bar, to join some detectives for the race and I saw them laughing together as I walked into the trainer's room.

"Set 'em up!" I said cheerily to the barman. "The whole bar. I've got Fine Cotton in this one and he'll go bloody close!"

"You've got Fine Cotton?" asked one of the trainers.

"That's right! The big plunge! Have one on me!"

"I reckon you're having one on us! You been pulling him up or something?" I smiled knowingly and they crowded around me, most of them with their money riding on our horse.

"And racing!" blared the monitor.

The race was run and finished in a swift blur of pictures and garble of sound. None of it made any sense amid the roar of voices and back slapping around me. I remembered hearing the name Fine Cotton more and more toward the end, and that it was a close finish, and ordering another beer, but the rest was a daze and I actually had to ask for assurance that my horse had won.

"What? Of course he won. What's the matter with you? It was a clear half head to Harbour Gold!"

"Well then, I'm the only bugger that did my job right."

The trainer stared after me as I drained the beer and stumbled out to claim my horse.

When Bold Personality won, John Dixon was parked next to a nearby golf course listening to the radio. He had jumped into the air and shouted "You bloody beauty!" to the amazement of a group of women teeing off a short distance away. Bobby North was watching Mally's moment of triumph from a safe distance up in the stand. John Gillespie was telling his detectives how much money he had won. And I walked into total chaos.

It was a disaster! People were running from everywhere to the winner's enclosure, where a pack of bookies' clerks were hollering at the stewards.

"Wrong horse! Wrong horse! Ring-in!" they shouted. "That's Bold Personality! Official inquiry! Ring-in!"

Cameras clicked, punters took down details of the horse's markings, press people were screaming for my statement and there was an ugly rumble from the crowd. Officials surrounded me demanding the horse's papers. I needed time to think.

"I'll just have to get the papers from the owners," I said. "I'll be right back."

Slowly I wandered to Personality's stall for a look in my blue bag. It was just an ordinary vinyl carrybag, a little ragged around the edges with wear, but vast sums of money now rode on its contents because it was faintly possible that when the uproar started, Gillespie had slipped the fake papers into it. And if I could offer the stewards something official, bogus or not, they might call correct weight on the race. A more detailed investigation would certainly follow, but correct weight meant all bets would be paid.

The bag was bare. The papers were missing and so was the Phantom. It was a doublecross of the highest order. A beauty! A top act! And I grinned, then sniggered, then laughed! No papers! Bloody hell! Was this going to cause a stir!

"The papers weren't in my bag," I told the Chief Steward. "I'll have to go look for the owners in the bar."

"Doesn't this horse look a bit lighter in colour than the last time you raced it?"

"Yes, it certainly does."

"Not that one, you idiot!" he said. "That's Harbour Gold. Yours is over there in the swabbing box!"

"Well, it was worth a try. See, I can't tell one horse from another!"

I searched through all the bars looking for a familiar face but North and Mally weren't around, Dixon was gone, and Silvertongue and the Phantom had vanished. Well, there was nothing for it but to have a beer! And hang around until correct weight on Harbour Gold so I could pick up my winnings. I was especially pleased about that, because Silvertongue had my car and I needed the money for cab fare. I ordered another beer and drained it in one hit. So what if the ring-in went wrong! It certainly wasn't my fault.

So much had happened so fast that a sudden crush of media people, filming and photographing, seemed like a perfectly natural progression. Then I saw Bobby North come in, and he sidled up to stand beside me, looking anywhere else and talking under his breath like a spy.

"Have you seen the others?" he whispered.

The loudspeakers blared: "Mr Malcolm MacGregor Lowndes and Miss Pauline Pearse, come to the Stewards Room please."

"Don't talk now. Catch up with you later," whispered North, and he hurried away.

It was the longest wait for correct weight in Australian racing history and it seemed even longer to me, standing in the open air bar expecting to be arrested at any moment. When it came, the announcement was like a thunderclap.

"All bets on Fine Cotton are to stand!"

The loudspeaker pronounced sentence and bookmakers' cash registers rang north to New Guinea, east to Fiji and west to Perth.

"Harbour Gold is declared the winner of race four!"

"You beauty!" I bellowed. "That's two hundred bucks and a taxi the hell out of here!"

But picking up my winnings was not without a few moments of embarrassment, the bookie regarding me with frank amazement.

"You're Haitana, aren't you? Don't tell me your money was on Harbour Gold! Hey fellers! Here's Haitana, the ring-in chappy! He was backing the bloody opposition!"

As I left the course, their laughter drifted after me.

After ducking through several pubs and changing cabs I arrived at North's house suddenly anxious to find out where Fine Cotton was. Standard criminal practice is to shoot the horse and bury it, and I wasn't going to wear that. But Bobby soon put me at ease.

"I ran into Dixon on the way home. I was travelling along the freeway at a fair clip when this little silver bullet pisses past with a float on the back, and it's Dixon. I had to flatten it to pull up beside him and flag him over. I told him to head west, anywhere west, just get the damn horse out of here." I looked out into the yard where, that same morning, there had been so much drama, hilarity, and hope.

"So what happens from here?"

Bobby had been speaking to the Phantom by telephone, and we were to meet at a pub on the way to the Gold Coast, so we hopped into Bob's car and sped south in silence. It was my first real chance to think about the doublecross and who was to blame, and the answer kept coming up Gillespie. Of course the fatal leak could have come from anywhere, but overriding everything was the Phantom's careless approach, and the missing papers. Of course it was only speculation and I doubted it would do any real good to raise the issue.

North and I strolled into the pub to find Gillespie casually arranged against the bar, grinning.

"Well, mate, I've got the next scam already organised for you," he said, after a sip of his beer, "and it's a good one too."

"Bullshit! Leave me out of it!" I protested, and the three of us fell about in stitches.

"You should have seen Silvertongue's face!" moaned Gillespie, doubled up with glee. "He was out of there so fast he didn't even wait to pick his gear up from your car, Hayden!"

"And what about Mally!" screamed North. "Standing up and shouting 'I've been in racing for twenty years and that's my horse!'"

"Good on the old bugger!" said Gillespie. "And Dixon! He'd driven the real Fine Cotton back inside the gates when he heard on the radio we were done. He probably kangaroo'd that car of his halfway home! And he's asking me 'How come we didn't get paid? We did win you know. Crooked bastards.'"

"Talk about confused!"

"I'll tell you what the real shame is, though," the Phantom said on a more serious note. "I had this horse called Kiwi Tradition running up at Rockhampton and we've been pulling the hell out of him for months. So today we were going to let him run and he was a sure thing, so I had organised to put every cent we won on Fine Cotton on him later in the afternoon. Would you believe it, the bastard bolted home at fourteen to one and we didn't have a thing to put on it!"

I stared in disbelief.

"You mean we had a certainty today? Apart from Cotton?"

"Yeah. Bloody shame, isn't it. Now listen, Hayden, I'll tell you what we're going to do to get out of this. John Dixon called and you'll never believe it. He's stashed Cotton at some place just over the road from the Police Academy. Now as it happens, the cops have taken Bold Personality to the Academy stables, so it's easy. We're going to swap them back. Tonight."

Without waiting for my reaction, he turned to Bobby.

"Find out who's on the gate at nights and see if we can buy him."

North shrugged.

"Well, anything's worth a try."

I was flabbergasted. If all went according to plan, the cops would wake to discover that Bold Personality, their prime piece of evidence, was himself a ring-in.

Chapter Twenty-two
THE PAY OFF

Every time my eyes strayed to John Dixon, I shuddered. It was a few days after the ring-in and we were all lying low while the media had a field day with the whole affair.

"If you're so worried about being recognised, John, why don't you change the colour of your hair?" North had suggested. And as there was still some dye left over from the Bold Personality job, they had used that. John Dixon was now sitting across the table from me at Bobby's place, his hair bright red, and while none of us enjoyed looking at it much, it sure attracted our attention.

Bobby was pacing and it made me nervous.

"What a balls up!" said the Phantom.

"And you say the cops still want their money?" asked Dixon. "Where are we going to get fifty bloody grand?"

"We'll need time," said North. "Bloody hell, I didn't even back the thing and now I've got to help fork out!"

The raid on the Oxley police barracks hadn't got past first base. The Phantom figured we had to hire some heavy boys to pull it off for us, and none were available—not to break into a police barracks. And with that option up the creek, Gillespie had called a council of war to figure out how we could escape the criminal charges which were almost certain to be laid against us. As always, it boiled down to money. He claimed the cops had assured him that if they were given the pay off they had been promised, we had nothing to worry about.

"Time is what we need, all right," he agreed. "If we can't raise the pay off within the next couple of weeks, I'd say we're in trouble."

"Well, what do you think?" asked North.

"Look, the only one they'll be after for questioning right now is Hayden," Gillespie said, "so if we're going to get some breathing space, say three weeks or so, Haitch and I better take off south and you and John Dixon can handle raising whatever cash you can from this end."

"Sounds fair enough," agreed Bobby. "We'll take the Gold Coast. At least until the heat dies down."

And so within twenty-four hours the Phantom and I were in Sydney, on the move in a big way, with a target of twenty-five grand. I'll admit it was curious being so closely in league with someone I was almost certain had pulled a doublecross, and I wasn't sure that it was worthwhile trying to buy our way out of trouble with the cops, but any route out of the Fine Cotton mess was worth a look and life with the Phantom was never dull.

Gillespie's first move was to make a direct approach to Silvertongue, offering to keep his name out of the whole mess if he'd pay off the cops for us in one big hit. It was by far the simplest answer to our financial woes, and I confronted him eagerly when he returned to our motel.

"How did you go? How was the reception?"

"A bit frosty, mate. He says we should be paying him for protection. He's a lost cause unless we can bring some pressure to bear somehow."

Gillespie looked at me as if it was my turn to make a suggestion. I ripped the top from another beer and shrugged.

"Beats me."

"You can see his point of view. Hundreds of thousands of dollars went down the tube on this one. No one is feeling generous. They're going to need encouragement."

"Got something in mind?"

"Well, as a matter of fact . . ."

The Phantom had something in mind, all right. He had already organised my appearance on the current affairs show, *Sixty Minutes*.

"There's a double pay off, Haitch," he explained. "I think we can squeeze ten grand out of the television people for an appearance fee, and then if you can just talk about being in fear of your life and so on — sound really scared — old Silvertongue might think twice."

"Why would he?"

"Think about it. If you can sound convincing enough he might believe you. He might believe you're terrified of getting knocked. And scared people do silly things like telling television people the full story. Now say you do get bumped . . ."

"Johnny!"

"No, say you did. Whoever gave you the treatment would have to be worried about how much you told the media and where it pointed. So it's insurance that way. And if you've got to the media once, who's to say you won't go back with the full story unless Silvertongue plays ball?"

"You don't think it will only upset him?"

"He's already upset."

It sounded good, and there was the money to think of, and with the Phantom you knew where you stood on money—nowhere!

The *Sixty Minutes* people were cautious, and first they sent a producer out to meet me at a hotel. Gillespie had already given them the "in fear of my life" routine, and I think the poor bugger who came out was scared witless. The arrangements were that I had to stand in front of a window where I was clearly visible at all times, otherwise Gillespie's "boys" would be in to find out what was wrong. The drama of it worked because they agreed to pay the money.

The next day I met the full crew at a motel and it turned into quite a party. I think they felt sorry for me as I spoke of my dire peril and dragged names of heavies out of the air. The interview lasted for two bottles of whisky, which meant I was late as hell for a rendezvous with the Phantom at a T.A.B. hotel in town, and he was getting edgy. I couldn't understand his nervousness unless someone really was trying to knock me.

"Haitch! Where have you been? I was getting worried!"

"Why? What's to worry about?"

"Oh. Nothing really."

I studied his face. It shone with sincerity. "See Hayden, I don't want anything to happen that I don't know about. I had two guys hanging around in a fake police car outside the motel. If there was trouble they were going to bowl in and say they were detectives. Put you under arrest. But they didn't call in, useless bastards!"

"Now you're getting me worried!"

I knew that as far as Silvertongue was concerned I would have to be in the clear on the ring-in, but the danger was that Gillespie could be using my name to set up a new con. Otherwise there was no reason for him to be worried about my safety.

"Come on, Johnny," I said, "no bull. What are you up to?"

"Now don't you worry about a thing, Haitch. You leave it to me! I think I can raise the rest of the money now. You just sit back and enjoy it!"

And there were some funny and enjoyable moments. My face had been splashed over every newspaper and television screen in the country and the police were looking for me for "questioning", so everyone who recognised me — and that was just about everyone — seemed to regard it as a special adventure. A few nights later at the private bar in our own motel we met a doctor out with his wife and friends for the night. It happened that this bar was the haunt of the higher echelons of Randwick's racing toffs, and the woman knew who I was straight away.

"That's Hayden Haitana!" she squealed, and every head turned.

John Gillespie and I were sitting alone at a table. A moment later the waiter turned up with a magnum of champagne and a note — "Compliments of Fine Cotton". We raised our glasses to the doctor, which broke the ice, and soon they had joined us — doctors, solicitors, and dentists, rubbing shoulders with crooks! I must say we took advantage of the situation, running up a huge bill and swapping jokes until the doctor stood up and demanded silence.

"My daughter is a psychiatrist," he thundered, "and I am a medical practitioner, and I have never met anyone more certifiably crazy than Hayden Haitana. Should he go to trial I shall defend him by saying he must go free on the grounds of insanity!"

It brought the house down and the doctor offered to buy the next round if he could order the concoction. It was a shocker, made of tequila, lemon, salt, cointreau, worcestershire sauce, half a dozen other mystery ingredients, and a whisky chaser, accompanied by his business card so that those who needed an antidote in the morning could consult him.

The next day we were gone, heading north to Brisbane, driving as far as northern New South Wales where the Phantom made a clandestine telephone call.

"That's the rest of our half of the fifty grand just come through," he said, climbing back into the car. "We'll have to go back to Sydney."

"Oh, well, that's great! What's the scheme?"

"It's the old story, Haitch. I'm pretty sure you wouldn't want to know." And the bugger is that cheeky he booked us into the same motel.

"Oh you're back," said the desk clerk. "That's good."

"Why? Because we spent so much dough?"

"No, no."

"What? Did the police eventually come around?"

"No, you left your suits in your room. Crazy bastards. I was going to flog them off as souvenirs!"

I could have taken it as a warning because eventually that faithful jacket of mine was souvenired, almost straight off my back, in a Brisbane courtroom. You can't trust anybody these days!

After we had made all the money John could wheedle, con and borrow in Sydney, we returned to Brisbane, to Bobby North's to compare notes with him and John Dixon. They had somehow managed to raise their half of the pay off, and there was an atmosphere of huge relief as the Phantom counted it and left for a meeting with his tame cops. I decided that a celebration was in order and got stuck into the beer, and Bob was full of cheek about how easy it was to get around the legal system. When the Phantom returned he was hailed as a conquering hero, and he accepted our praise with typical modesty.

"So we're in the clear now?" I slurred. "It's all over?"

"Well, there'll be no trouble from the cops in court, that's for sure!" beamed Gillespie.

"What? What court? What are you talking about?" gasped Bobby. "I thought that if we weighed in it was all sweet."

"Oh no," said the Phantom, as if the terms of the arrangement had been quite clear. "We'll all be charged. It's just that there won't be any real evidence against us. These copper mates of mine will steer it wrong."

"Jesus, John, are you sure? I thought you said we weren't even going to be charged!" moaned Bob. "Now these mates of yours have got our money and we've got nothing left to bargain with. We should have kept half to give to them afterward! Are you sure you can trust them?"

"You sure all that money isn't in the John Gillespie retirement fund?" I laughed and Gillespie joined in, just a fraction too late.

"We'll be sweet. You just wait and see!"

Chapter Twenty-three
FAME

My face stared at me from a newspaper flyer and the headline read "Ring-in Trainer Missing". A pimply country youth had just finished filling my car with juice and he joined me outside the battered service station shop.

"That's you, hey?"

"That's right. Do I look missing to you?"

"Nah. But if someone was to arst, I'd say you went the other way."

We laughed about that and I pulled my wallet out to pay, but he raised his hand.

"Don't worry 'bout it, Hayden. Just give us your autograph instead, will ya?"

The entire journey had been like that, ever since the Phantom sent me packing with instructions to stay well under cover. As we spoke about the ins and outs of the pay off deal at Bobby North's that day, the terms and conditions had kept on coming until both Bobby and I figured we had probably been conned, by the cops, if not by Gillespie. They had given instructions that the only way I could avoid arrest and jail in the very near future was to lie extra low so that I didn't look too cocky about it. So that afternoon I was halfway back to Adelaide to spend what time I had left with my wife and family.

And it was glorious. Monica, the kids and I set off on a driving holiday along the South Australian and Victorian coastlines, staying at caravan parks. We tried hard to stay clear of the public eye as the ring-in controversy raged in the press. But as I had discovered on the trip south, travelling incognito was next to impossible.

At first we were using the driver's licence of a friend for identification—a bloke called White—but after a while we gave it away as useless. The first stop we made, after Monica had booked in under the fake name, the caretaker confronted me where I was playing with the kids in the pool.

"Gidday, Hayden!" he said. "How you getting on with Mrs White? Get out of there and come and have a beer with us!"

A few things hit home on that journey. My sweet little eight-year-old girl Mandy couldn't understand why we had to change our identity, but when someone asked her name she was solid as a trooper.

"You'll have to ask my dad. It might be Mary, but it might not be too." I laughed at the time, but it didn't feel too crash hot.

The holiday lingered on, every moment more precious for our having no idea when it would end. I had every intention of turning myself over to the Queensland police as soon as a warrant for my arrest was issued, and when at last the news came over the radio I pulled the car over to the side of the highway, turned, and headed west. At first I couldn't bring myself to speak, but Monica's eyes were on me.

"Time to pack you and the kids off home," I said, staring straight ahead, but Monica was quite resigned.

"All good things . . ." she said, and we each made a silent pledge not to talk about the future. The drive home was mostly silent, and the kids, sensing the mood, were extra good.

It was in Mildura, well into the trip back to Brisbane, that I had a brainstorm. What the hell was I doing with the family car when Monica was going to need it? Covered in smiles, delighted by any excuse to delay the inevitable, I threw a U-turn and hit the pub. First up, I worked out how much I needed for airfare, and an afternoon raid on the T.A.B. looked after that. In fact I did so well that I was flush with drinking funds, and a homeward pub crawl seemed in order. And every hotel was the same—a warrant for my arrest was far more serious than being wanted for questioning, but no one was going to dob me in. I tried in vain to explain that I wasn't really in hiding, but no one wanted to listen and I was spirited into the darker corners of bars, safe from prying eyes. No one talked, and I got a fair way before my car gave me away.

The cops had got word that my battered old Holden was headed south-west and a roadblock was set up at Truro. I was drinking there at the local with two old racing friends, full of booze, when news of the ambush filtered through. I was in enough trouble without going for drink driving again, and the car was parked right outside, so I figured the police had to cotton on sooner or later.

"May the cops be my taxi!" I shouted, and ordered another round.

Right at that moment they swarmed in, a whole crew, as though I was armed and dangerous, and believe it or not they had the place surrounded! A cop sauntered straight over to me.

"Are you Hayden Haitana?"

I thought he was kidding.

"Yes, I am," I agreed, then turned to my drinking companions. "This guy must need glasses!"

"There is a warrant for your arrest regarding allegations in Queensland."

"Yes, righto. I'll come quietly," I grinned. "At least I'll get my fare to Queensland on the house!"

They loaded me into the police car and took me to a neighbouring town with the ridiculous name of Nurioopta, charged and fingerprinted me, then locked me up in an interrogation room. I could hear them talking next door, and by standing on the table and pushing a ceiling panel up, I saw that they were searching my blue race bag. Despite the booze I felt instant panic, because books containing damning notes and all my money were stored in a false bottom. Somehow I had to stop them, and the only way I could think of was diversion. I pushed the panel of ceiling right out and dived over the dividing wall, crashing straight through the ceiling next door and down on top of the police.

I lay on the floor between their desks, and as their faces stared down at me I became hysterical. I had never seen anything so funny in all my life. Reinforcements rushed in from everywhere. I was dragged to my feet and thrown into a proper cell, and that's where the fun really started because one of the officers looked in on me and shook his head with a half-smile.

"You won't get out of this one."

"Bullshit!" I thundered back.

A tiny grate cemented into the ten foot ceiling was the only object I thought I could damage. With a flying leap from a wood-slab I grabbed the bars of the grate, wrenching down with all my weight and strength. The surrounds caved in, the grate bent, and I crashed to the floor, broken cement cascading around me. I barely had time to arrange myself neatly on the bunk when the boys in blue burst in.

"Holy Mother of Christ! How did you manage that?"

"Manage what?"

I spent the remainder of my stay in another cell, stripped to my underpants, hands secured behind my back, under constant guard. But once I had sobered up I got on well enough with my captors and a few days later, when Monica came down to pick up my gear, they explained I had presented them with an interesting problem.

"We can't charge him with attempted escape because he was actually trying to break in, so we've charged him with wilful damage. Do you think he'll pay restitution?"

When I appeared in court on the wilful damage charge, the magistrate made it clear that he wasn't going to fine me whichever way I pleaded, so to get it over with I pleaded guilty and agreed to pay the hundred and forty dollars restitution for damage to the cells.

"Do you need time to pay, Mr Haitana?" he asked.

"What time does the T.A.B. open, Your Worship?"

The court exploded, the magistrate rolled his pencil from the desk so that no one would see him laughing along, and the case was closed.

And I was off to Adelaide Jail, to wait for my extradition to Queensland to be arranged. It was a simple enough process, a short paddy-wagon ride from the police cells to prison, but my short holiday from the media spotlight had left me unprepared for the riot which ensued. Press and the public jammed the road, bringing the wagon to a complete halt, and I had to stay safe inside until a path could be cleared through the throng.

"Here he comes! Here he comes!" they screamed as I walked through protective columns of prison guards.

I wondered what on earth had hit me, and wondered still further when I found myself shoved in with the prison's tough boys. I couldn't understand why a simple con like me deserved that kind of classification. Then after two days I was transferred to an even more security-conscious yard, with the worst of the State's criminals and those who had been threatened by other prisoners — a section where security was so strict that whoever cooked the food was made to taste it at random in case broken glass or some kind of poison was included on the menu. All showers had the doors removed and I was constantly under surveillance, sometimes by female warders, what's more! How can you scrub your bum properly in mixed company? I had never encountered anything like that kind of jail environment, and I began to curse the day I told *Sixty Minutes* that my life was under threat.

Far from dying away, attention from the outside only increased. I was told that the prison switchboard was jammed for days with callers offering support, wanting hot race tips, and offering to represent me in court. There was even a call from my mother in New Zealand. And then Monica was on the blower, upset by intense media harassment. She said she was having to leap the back fence just to go shopping, and was forced to escort the kids to school.

I saw red on that one and wanted to call the editors of every media group in town, but as I was allowed only one telephone call a day, a personal approach was impractical . . . or was it? When my turn at the telephone came the following day I decided to maximise impact by calling talkback radio. At the time, the prison authorities had no idea that my voice was being broadcast right across South Australia, but it sure did the trick. The disc jockey came to the party in a big way, and sounded like he was in ecstasy as I got straight to the point.

"Could you use your influence to stop the media bothering Monica?"

"Surely it's not our staff," he said, "or any ethical journalist I know? I'll get on it right away."

"Well, in return I'll gladly speak to the media when I get out, but for heaven's sake just get them off my family's back!"

"Okay, Hayden. Mate, is there anything else I can do for you?"

"Sure, send half a dozen taxis down to the prison, will you? There's a few boys want to get out of here!"

I had quite forgotten about Bainsey's relationship with the Adelaide taxi drivers and it was the wrong joke to pull. Soon half a dozen of the buggers had parked outside the gate, putting the prison administration onto me right away. But it was worth the dressing-down because my media appeal had the desired effect and brought Monica some peace.

Of course, the press doesn't give up that easily and some elements turned their talents to deceit. Through Monica I had warned my mother not to speak to newspapers but being in her late seventies and a simple, trusting soul, she was easily tricked. One afternoon she telephoned me from New Zealand and we had been speaking for a while when I suggested the cost might be getting a little high.

"Oh no, love," she said. "Some nice man from the newspaper is paying for it."

"It's not going through their switchboard, is it?"

"Oh . . . I think so, dear."

"Bye bye, Mum."

I was astounded by their gall. They had listened to every word and published most of the information a few days later.

After ten days in Adelaide I was extradited to Queensland. Two Consorting Squad Detectives came down for the pick-up. I was by now used to media interest but our reception in Brisbane came as a terrible fright to the D's. When we arrived at the airport the cameras were there in incredible force, right out on the tarmac where there was no escape.

"Sorry, Hayden," one of them said. "We better put the handcuffs back on to make it look good, okay?"

We had to shove hard to make our way through the pack, the detectives angry and tightlipped, each of us stumbling and staggering as we tried to avoid tripping over cables and walking, face first, into lenses. The detective I was handcuffed to and I were pulled painfully away from each other as we climbed into a car and waited for our luggage. Cameramen bounced on the bonnet trying to film through the windscreen, reporters jammed microphones into the side of my face and for the first time in my life I felt sorry for politicians and police.

And if the airport was difficult, the next day was worse. I was due to appear in Brisbane Magistrates Court, and it was bedlam. The police car pushed its way through press and spectators into the security of the court car park but even that wasn't enough. A solid steel door had to be opened for us to drive through into the building. Then when the police arrived in the courtroom it was packed so tightly there was no way they could hold the hearing there. It was shifted to another court, then yet another, and I was whisked upstairs and downstairs as elevators were turned off to stall the newshounds. The cops said they had never seen that scale of mayhem in court.

At that time, Gillespie, North and Dixon had already been charged with conspiracy, and Dixon also in connection with the dud cheque he had passed to Bill Naoum. North and Gillespie had given themselves up and Dixon fully intended to, but typically, the poor bugger was cornered and arrested before he had the chance. North had given him twenty grand to put into his cheque account to cover the cost of Bold Personality, and save him going for fraud, and after depositing the money, Johnny had walked straight into the arms of waiting police.

All of them were free on bail, but the magistrate set mine at fourteen thousand dollars cash, so into Brisbane prison I went, and there I stayed until I was extracted by the Phantom to the animal roar of my fellow inmates, in the stuffy boot of a solicitor's tiny car. That, I suppose, is the price of fame!

Chapter Twenty-four
The Fall Out

"Hey, Johnny," I said, to break the silence, "how come you set up the media outside the jail this morning, and then the solicitor said you'd changed your mind and I had to leave in the boot?"

"Oh that! Well, see, now we've whetted their appetite. I was watching across the road and they were mean as cats when they missed you! Next thing we up the price for another exclusive interview and they'll be beating the door down to show each other up."

"Before or after Cairns?"

"Yes. Well, what does everybody think about it? You in, Bobby?"

North raised his eyes from a glass of tomato juice and shook his head. "No. Not a ring-in. Count me out."

"Johnny D.?"

"I'm with Bob."

"But you're in, eh, Hayden?"

I looked at him for a moment, the man with whom I had gone through so much havoc, who had maybe doublecrossed us, whose friends were invisible cops and stewards that had to be paid off, who had just bailed me out of jail and who was now calling the favour.

"I don't think so, John," I drawled. "I wouldn't mind heading back to Adelaide to see Monica before the trial. I can always go legal aid if we can't afford a private solicitor."

"Well then, that's that," said the Phantom. "We'll think of something else. Right now I think we'd better have another drink, hey?"

I returned to Adelaide, reporting twice weekly to police and staying free of the Phantom's influence until the commital hearings, which were still nearly six months away. I had planned to take it easy, find a part-time job, and settle down into a proper family routine for a change. Naturally, John Gillespie had other ideas.

Still very much in the public eye, I had been asked to do several unpaid charity appearances and was happy enough to go along for a good cause, but when the Phantom heard about it on the news he was outraged.

"Haitch, get back up!" he shouted into the telephone. "There's a fortune to be made on promotion work here! There's a media guy on the Gold Coast just dying to get his hands on you!"

"I hope he's not queer," was all I could think of to say.

"Piss off, Haitch. This is serious business."

"Yeah, but it's no go. I've got to report to police twice a week, remember?"

"No, that's all right. We need you here tomorrow and I've got you booked on the seven o'clock flight out of Adelaide."

"But like I said, I've got to report to the cops tomorrow, and the conditions are non-negotiable."

"Say you're sick!" urged the Phantom. "Or better still, report just after midnight. That's tomorrow, isn't it? Do that!"

So I did. I made the flight still unsure of what Gillespie had in mind and, quite frankly, beyond caring. I was met in Brisbane by a local television channel's news team and driven halfway down to the Gold Coast, where two current affairs teams from the same network were waiting with the Phantom and his media man. During the drive, with only mild curiosity, I had asked if anyone knew what was happening and the reporter had looked at me very strangely.

"You're producing Fine Cotton."

"Fair dinkum. What about the cops?"

"We're filming first and then you're going to hand it over to the police. And then they're going to give it back to you. You're planning to use it to raise money for charity." He paused. "Aren't you?"

"What charity?" I asked, but I knew what charity all right. The Gillespie retirement fund kind of charity.

Gillespie and his Gold Coast contact had made a deal with the network for exclusive reports, and had already fetched Fine Cotton from wherever he was stashed. When I first saw him he was standing in the middle of a paddock with his head down, and even from that distance I could tell that my old mate was in a shocking condition. When they got a close look, the reporters were outraged, and they were going to make it hot for me on that one!

Each of the three crews was under the impression that their own programmes had the story alone, and as each was paying a different amount they had begun brawling among themselves. The only way out of the jam was to offer them three different angles on the same story, which is harder than it sounds.

As Fine Cotton had a bad case of Queensland itch I gave one news crew a "neglected ring-in" angle and variations of a "life under threat" story to the others. By then I was so confused about what I was supposed to be saying I mixed up the interviews badly.

I was livid, but there's no point in ranting at the Phantom and I did get my own back. The charity deal he had set up was in aid of a sad medical case and I was so sure he was going to grab at least some of the money for himself that I found out where donations should really go, and gave the proper address during the interviews. Gillespie didn't say anything about it, but I did end up having to borrow money to pay my own fare back to Adelaide.

About this time my reporting conditions were removed and I shifted up to Queensland where I could be in close touch with legal aspects of the committal hearings. I drove up from Adelaide with Monica and the kids to treat them to a holiday on the Gold Coast — to the delight of the Phantom, who was by now up to incredible mischief, mostly involving the unauthorised use of my name and other people's credit cards. When we were seen in public together his schemes gained much greater credibility, and he took full advantage of my company.

But I didn't want Gillespie involved in any arrangements for my family, so I had booked a caravan for the three days we could honestly afford — three days of blissful, non-conspiratorial peace. But on the very first night, when all of us were asleep, there was a knock on the door.

"Wake up, Hayden!" shouted the Phantom. "What are you doing in this? We've got you a penthouse booked!"

"John? I hate to ask what the hell you're up to!"

"Come and have a look at this!"

Wearily, I dragged on some jeans and went off with him to check it out. And lo and behold, it was bloody brilliant!

It was some millionaire's pad and it had everything we couldn't possibly afford — three swimming pools, saunas, three bedrooms, two bathrooms, right on the beachfront — the works.

"Nothing's too good for my mate Haitch!" smiled Gillespie.

And despite my wonder at the luxury, I felt a cold shudder run down my spine.

"Listen, Monica!" I was soon shaking her awake. "We've got a shack down the beach we can move into right away!"

"Mmuhh?" she said. "Has it got a bathroom?"

"I want to stay here!" piped up Mandy. "It's got a swimming pool!"

"Shhh!" I whispered. "Don't tell Mummy but this place has got two hot pools and a cold one."

Monica's face was a picture when, at two o'clock in the morning, she found herself in heaven with hot and cold running everything. The refrigerator was stuffed with food and beer and the kids had a different bed for every day of the week. John Gillespie was his usual modest self.

"Courtesy of the Phantom," he said.

Those were the ten most wonderful days of our lives. No expense was spared, everything was on room service and the telephone bill ran to about eight hundred dollars. And it was also the beginning of the end of the Fine Cotton crew, because the Phantom was pushing his luck too far.

What could I say when I discovered that the whole thing had gone on John Dixon's credit card? Poor John was off on some wild goose chase for Gillespie at the time, and had no idea how high everyone else was living at his expense. Bobby North was in the same boat, continually running up expenses on one deal or another for the Phantom — he even paid for an overseas trip Gillespie was giving someone — and trusting Gillespie's promise that a heap of money was due in from Switzerland any day now.

The days stretched and still there was no money. And there were rumours circulating that North was tied up in some heavy deals, when he certainly was not. Someone was using his name, and we didn't need much of an I.Q. to guess who. But all of us desperately wanted to trust Gillespie, and we convinced ourselves that, whatever he was up to, it would eventually work out in our interests. It is a tribute to the personal magnetism of the man.

But our illusions were finally, totally shattered a month or so later, when right out in the open, he ripped us off for the Fine Cotton movie.

It was February 1985, I had returned to Adelaide, and the committal hearings were just around the corner. The Phantom called with the news.

"Hey, Haitch! Want to be a movie star? There are some blokes interested in talking to you."

"But if we tell them what really happened, they might blow the whistle!"

"No. I've checked them out and they're okay. We've already told them everything anyway. But listen, they're paying good money and all of us are going to donate our shares to buy you a house on the Gold Coast. There's a movie contract waiting for you to sign, so get up here! I've already arranged your transport to bring you up for the committalls, so just change the ticket." But the airline knew nothing, Gillespie wasn't answering, and by then I had barely enough time to make the hearings by road.

I left Adelaide that afternoon in a cloud of dust to travel via Sydney, but the car played up twice and by the time I made Randwick I was flat broke. The Phantom was still in limbo and the only contact I could make anywhere was his Gold Coast media man.

"But Gillespie said he wired the money off!" he said. "He's flush because they've just picked up an advance on the movie and Gillespie is holding your share. He's already sent it. The lot."

"That's bullshit! Listen, it's Saturday, right? I've got to be in Brisbane Monday and I'm broke. You put the airfare in my T.A.B. betting account yourself—now!"

He was a pretty reliable sort of bloke so I headed down to the T.A.B. to wait for the credit to come through. I waited for hours, and when the teller shook her head for the fifteenth frustrating time, I dashed back to a telephone.

"What do you mean, 'what happened'?" Gillespie's man was confused.

"Where's the fucking money?"

"It should be there by now. I ran into Gillespie on the way and he said he was going straight down to the club so I gave it to him."

"Oh, Jesus! On no!"

I was desperate. If I didn't make the opening day that fourteen thousand dollars bail was up in smoke and I was back in the slammer.

"You come home with me, love," said the barmaid. "You can stay at my place tonight." I had just drunk my last dollar and the woman had pitied me.

"It'll cost you," I said, and blow me down if she didn't take me up on it! Next morning I roared out of Sydney with just enough petrol money to make Brisbane, and arrived barely in time for court. And when I got there, the Phantom appeared puzzled.

"Where have you been, Haitch?"

The committal hearings were split into two separate sessions because the first ran over time, and it was during the few months between them that the bond between the four of us disintegrated totally. The movie script was well underway and that brought us back together to relive the frantic, heady days of the Fine Cotton ring-in, but the Phantom was handling the financial side of it and inevitably I was ripped off totally, and North and Dixon lost out to a certain extent too.

"Don't you worry about it, Haitch," Gillespie had said, pocketing all of my next instalment and handing a few thousand dollars of their shares to North and Dixon. "It's all going toward your house and you'll just spend it. You just pick out a nice place down the Gold Coast and I'll look after the rest."

So like a mug I spent my last two hundred dollars for deposit on a house and lost it as soon as the first payment was due. We had tried desperately to get in touch with Gillespie, because Dixon and Bobby needed more of their money too, for legal fees, and Bobby had some tough questions about the use of his name in a couple of big scams on the Coast, but the Phantom was out to lunch.

The final element of real suspense in the Fine Cotton drama rested on whether the Phantom would front for the next committal hearings. I believed he would because he had even offered to pick me up on his way from the Gold Coast, but as time grew short on the morning of the opening day, I knew him well enough to call a cab. The ghost had walked.

Chapter Twenty-five
MANDY

It is hard to be clear about my feelings for John Gillespie. I think I almost always knew what was going on in his mind and was able to disregard most of his failings — and I liked him very much for his cheek, for his grin, and for my own suspicion that somehow, who knows how, he always meant me to come out on top. Whether or not he ever intended the Fine Cotton ring-in to succeed will no doubt remain a mystery, but I am certain that he made a killing on it somehow — that he twisted that scam as far as it would twist until, for him alone, it became a mortal lock. Perhaps if I had agreed to go along with his plans for another ring-in it would have been different. Even now I might have been sharing some new adventure and maybe even some of the Fine Cotton spoils.

But for the Phantom that was the cut off point because he is a man who can't take no for an answer. When North, Dixon and I dared to bail out of his Cairns scheme that day at the pub, I remember that he took the rejection a touch too easily. And when, after a few months, we didn't find ourselves roped into it against our wills, it should have spelled out the fact that the Phantom no longer regarded us as mates, but as fair game.

Each of us had our own reasons for walking out and mine was my daughter Mandy. I remembered the time we were holidaying on the Gold Coast, my family sitting down to breakfast in an open-air restaurant. I had been amazed because for the first time Mandy had ordered something other than ice-cream.

"I'll have sausages and eggs please, and a cup of tea," she said to the waiter, feeling very grown up.

"Oh, damn!" said Monica. "There's channel something or the other over there getting their camera out."

"Just ignore them. They'll have to wait."

But when I turned back to my daughter there were tears streaming down her face.

"Do we have to run again, Daddy? Do I have time to eat my breakfast?"

The golden moment was lost but the memory was what gave me the strength, when the time came, to say no to another con.

For my life as a rogue, man, I can only say that I had a good time when the good times rolled. And above all, I can say I met the master of the art. Even when he ripped me off for most of my share of the movie, and I knew quite well what was going on, he had refused to be ruffled. We were in his car, driving away from a meeting with the film people at a city hotel, and he grinned his maddening grin as I clapped him on the shoulder and bellowed: "Johnny? You just ripped me off! Again!"

With thousands of dollars of mine stashed in the safety of his inside coat pocket the Phantom turned those pale blue eyes on me.

"Just practising, mate," he said. "Just practising."